VISUAL GUIDE TO
LOCK PICKING

3*rd* Edition

standard publications, inc.

Third Edition

3.0

Visual Guide to
Lock Picking

Authors
Mark McCloud
Gonzalez de Santos

Illustration
Mirko Jugurdzija

Editors
Jin Fujiwara
Lynard Richmar

standard publications, inc.

Cover design: **Mano Kime**
Layout editor: **Hori Hashimoto**
Production editor: **Rene Isaacs**
Manufacturing Producer: **Standard Publications, Inc.**

Copyright ©2006 by Standard Publications, Inc.
Standard Publications, Inc.
Champaign, Illinois 61825

The publisher offers discounts on this book when ordered in bulk quantities.

ISBN 0-9709788-6-3

Printed in the United States of America

Standard Publications, Incorporated

www.standardpublications.com

Excerpt from the 1832 edition of the Edinburgh Encyclopædia

LOCK is a well known instrument used for securing doors, chests, &c. and preventing them from being opened without a proper key. The simple and common lock, consists of a strong bolt, which is generally fitted into a case of metal, so as to admit of a motion backwards and forwards. The bolt should be inclosed on all sides, in such a manner as to prevent any access to it, except by a small opening, through which the key is to be introduced to withdraw it ; which opening should be surrounded inside the lock, by numerous wards or pieces of metal, forming a crooked and inter- rupted passage, to prevent the introduction of any improper instrument or false key, to pick the lock and withdraw the bolt. ... Indeed, an ill-disposed person might provide himself with a bunch of keys, called skeleton keys, which would open almost any lock constructed upon the above principles. A skeleton key means one which is cut out, so as to leave only the extreme part of the bit entire which moves the bolt, the other part being reduced to a thin piece, of just sufficient strength to move the bolt without breaking. It will easily be seen, that such a key would not be likely to meet with any interruption from wards, as very little solid metal is left. ...

In order to produce a lock free from these objections, many inge- nious mechanics have turned their attention to the subject of lock-making. In fact, the object of securing property from the depredations of others is so important, that few instruments have had more pains and ingenuity bestowed on them than locks.

Most of the contrivances for locks were supposed to possess some particular advantage, such as strength to resist violence, or security against being picked. Some speculators have acted upon a different principle alto- gether—that of attaching an alarm, a large bell, a species of fire-arms, &c. to a lock, in such a manner that an attempt to violate the lock would set the bell a-ringing, or discharge the fire-arms ; thereby causing a great noise and confusion, that the depredator might not escape. Our limits will not permit us to enter into the details of all the schemes that have been proposed to give security to locks ; but we shall notice principally such as have come into use by their own recommendation. ...

The subject of locks is so very extensive, that it would far exceed our limits to give a description of all the different forms and arrangements that have been proposed by various persons. (J. F.)

Contents

Introduction

Before you read any further you must first realize that lock picking is an art form. You should approach learning this art like you would any other. You may not be successful at first, but with time and dedication it can be mastered. Like most learned skills, lock picking takes practice. Lots of it. This book presents the various methods and techniques used in picking locks, along with the necessary tools. In order to better pick or bypass your locks it helps to understand how they work. That is why this book also provides a detailed and illustrated explanation of how the various locks actually work. You will find there are many times when this knowledge will be invaluable when learning or in the field.

The actual methods of lock picking are really quite simple. You are just exploiting the design of the lock in order to open it without the key. Applying these techniques, however, can prove to be quite difficult. As you practice, you will find that a lock that used to take you an hour to pick might now only take you ten minutes. A lock that used to take you five minutes might now only take you a few seconds. As you practice these skills, you will become much more efficient.

This book does not go into detail on the legal implications of lock picking. You are responsible for determining your own local laws and regulations. If you are using this book as a textbook in a course please ask your instructor any questions you may have. Do not do anything illegal. Period. You will find that there are many legitimate times when having the ability to pick locks is very useful. Beyond the many professional locksmiths around the country who make a good living doing legitimate lock picking, the skill of lock picking is useful for many professions. Law enforcement officers, emergency personnel, magicians, repossessors, and others are often called upon to pick locks in their professional line of duty.

Always keep in mind why you are picking any particular lock, and realize that there is often a better way to bypass it, which may ignore the lock completely.

1

Warded Locks

Warded Locks

Warded locks are probably one of the oldest types of locks in existence. In modern days, warded locks are obsolete for most purposes. Because they are so easy to pick, they do not provide much security. Despite this, they are still very useful and better than nothing at all.

Warded locks became popular throughout the Roman era. For many centuries, guilds tightly controlled lock technology from exactly how they were made to who could apprentice and learn about locks. Warded locks were a standard during this time. To improve security, ancient Chinese and Russians resorted to concealing the keyhole in elaborate artwork in the hope of increasing the security of their warded locks. The immense scale of some important locks provided an extra measure of security and made them harder to pick. Medieval Europeans went so far as to add hand and finger traps that would capture or amputate limbs of those who would dare insert the wrong key or tamper with the locking mechanism. These continued to be common in the early part of the twentieth century in many applications, including door locks.

Identifying Warded Locks

Today, warded locks can be found on cheaper padlocks, furniture, handcuffs, and luggage. If the *keyhole* somewhat resembles one of these figures on the right, then it is most likely a warded lock. The keys for this type of lock will generally slide in and out with almost no friction or

Example warded keyways

resistance. Most importantly, there will be no pins or wafers visible when looking inside the keyway.

How Warded Locks Work

When opening a lock, the goal is usually to rotate, move, or somehow actuate the *locking bolt*. This locking bolt, in turn, frees the shackle, deadbolt, or other retaining mechanism.

Let us begin by considering a simplified locking mechanism. This would consist of a *keyway,* the hole the key is inserted into, and a locking bolt that is turned by the key's *bit*. The figures below demonstrate this type of lock.

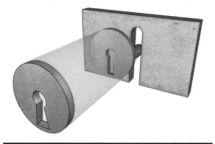

Simple lock - locked

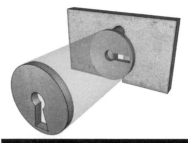

Simple lock - unlocked

Warded locks take this concept one step further. They have a set of *wards* inside the lock. Wards are simply obstructions that get in the way of any key other than the correct one(s). This means that all keys for a particular type of warded lock have the same bit for rotating the locking bolt. They also have *notches* arranged to avoid the wards of its particular lock. Different keys will have different notches; each one is specifically designed for its own lock. The correct

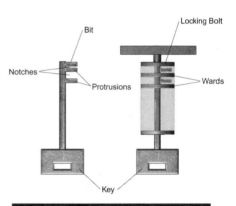

Parts of Warded lock

key will work simply because it has notches that line up with the wards, and it is allowed to rotate freely. Since each lock has the wards in a different location and the notches have to line up appropriately, only the correct key will, theoretically, open the lock.

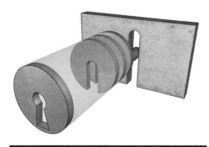

Warded lock - locked

Warded lock - unlocked

Example Warded Padlock

Warded padlocks are not nearly as common as their pin tumbler counterparts. They can, however, still be found all over the place, including your local hardware store. At a glance, they might even appear the same as a pin tumbler padlock, except for their lower price. Upon closer inspection by a trained eye, they are obviously inferior locks. We'll walk you through the operation of the common warded padlock, so you can better understand how they work, and how they are opened.

One way to identify a warded padlock is by its distinctive keyhole. The keyhole is often made of a small, free-spinning disk with a jagged hole cut into it. This hole acts as a type of ward. Only a key with the appropriate profile and shape can pass through it. The security provided by this design is quite minimal, and you will find many tools that can easily pass through the keyhole wards.

As you can see in the picture below, the padlock is constructed from many metal slabs stacked on top of each other and held in place with four rods. Most of the slabs simply provide three holes: two for the shackle and one for the key through which to pass. Some of them, however, are specifically designed to serve special purposes. For example, instead of a round keyway, some of the slabs have a flat slit that only allow the key to pass through, but not turn. These slabs act as wards. The key can easily pass through them as you insert it into the lock. But, if you try to turn the key, the ward will prevent it from rotating, unless the key is cut thin enough at that point to rotate in the slot. Different key combinations can be made simply by rearranging the ward slabs in the stack.

Warded Padlock

Keyway Wards

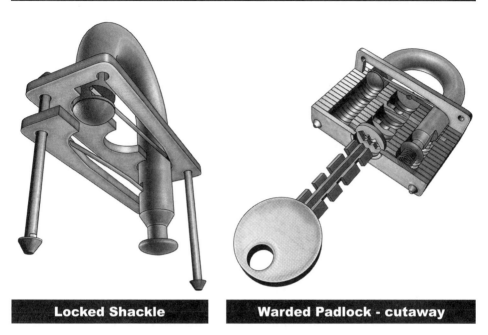

Locked Shackle   **Warded Padlock - cutaway**

Now we will take a closer look inside the lock for a better understanding of how it works. In this example, two of the slabs are special and provide the actual locking mechanism. The picture above shows just those two slabs and how they hold the shackle in place. Each of them contains a piece of spring metal that rests in a notch in the shackle. As long as this small piece of metal is in the notch, the shackle cannot be raised and will remain in the lock. The key, or other tool, simply bends this metal spring out of the way. Once it has cleared the notch, the shackle is free to leave the lock and another spring will pop the shackle out. It is important to note that this lock has two metal pieces locking the shackle in place, one on each side of the shackle. The lock will not open unless both metal pieces are moved out of the way simultaneously.

This complete cutaway view demonstrates how everything fits together. The warded and locking slabs have been shaded to demonstrate their internal arrangement. You can see how they can be rearranged to require a different key. Each side of the shackle has a metal spring holding it in place on opposite sides of the lock. One side of the key needs to push the metal spring down, while another portion of the key needs to push the other metal spring up.

As the key is inserted into the padlock, the shape of the keyway is designed to ensure that only the appropriate style of key will be used. From observing the cutaway view, though, you can see that this shape of hole is only present at the very entrance of the keyway; and you will be able to find many other tools, or even keys, that fit through. Almost any flat, metal object will be able to do this.

If the key is inserted only partway into the lock, the protrusions of the key blade may collide with the wards when you attempt to rotate it. As you can see in the first picture below, there is a ward that prevents the key from turning. It is large enough to allow the key to be inserted in one orientation, but not turn. The key may sometimes be placed partway into the lock, such that its notches line up with incorrect wards, allowing it to turn freely. However, the key's bits may then not be in the correct position to move the springs holding the shackle in place. Thus, it is important that your key not only has no protrusions that get in the way of the wards, but that it also has bits in the necessary locations. It may also need to have more than one bit, such as in this example. Some locks only require a bit at the end of the key, some don't. The tip of the key is not the only possible location for the necessary bit. Some warded locks will also have even stranger ward shapes in an effort to provide extra security.

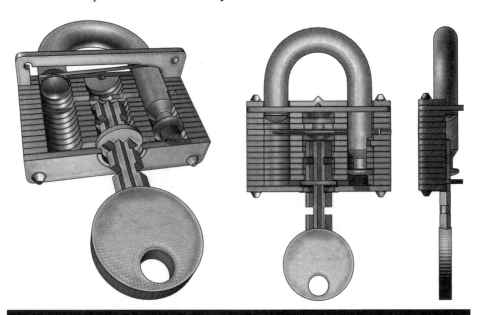

Key partially inside Warded Padlock

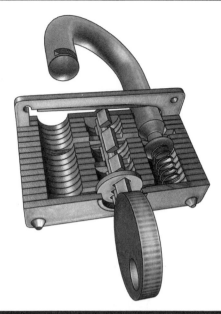

Warded Padlock - unlocked

When the proper key is fully inserted and rotated, it will depress both metal pieces out of the notches in the shackle. The shackle thus becomes free to pop out of the lock and rotate. There is usually a spring inside the lock that will push the shackle out for you automatically. This particular example of a padlock has such a spring. There is even a special slab that has a protrusion that keeps the shackle from flying out of the padlock when it is unlocked. Most common padlocks have a similar mechanism that keeps the shackle connected to the padlock, even when it is unlocked.

Shackle down

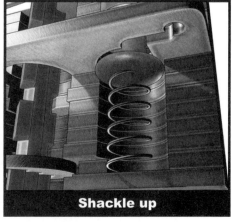

Shackle up

Picking Warded Locks

Picking warded locks is relatively quite simple. All you need to do is move the locking bolt. Unfortunately, there will be wards in your way. The easy way to handle wards is by simply avoiding them. If your key doesn't have any metal protrusions that get in the way of the wards, then the wards won't stop it from turning. So, let's look back at the simple lock design we described earlier. Let's make a key with just a *stem* and a *bit*. The bit is used to turn the locking bolt. There are no obstructions on the stem to get in the way of the wards. This key would have only the bare minimum amount of metal needed to make it work. Because of this, they are called *skeleton keys.*

So, the best way to pick a warded lock is to have a collection of skeleton keys for the various types of warded locks. Try each one in your set on the lock. Insert the key as far as you can and attempt to turn it. If it doesn't work, try moving it around slightly, and then move on to the next one. Making your own keys is also easy when using the impressioning method described later. Depending on the type and shape of the warded lock, you will need an appropriate skeleton key. There are sets of common skeleton keys that locksmiths can use successfully in most situations. Often, nothing more than a simple bent wire or L shaped tool is needed to manipulate the lock open.

It is interesting to note that most handcuffs in use today also utilize the warded lock. These devices are specifically adopted to restrain physical movement. Those that see regular use must be durable as well as cost-effective. In normal use the wrist clasp can simply be closed and ratcheted shut. The only way to open it is to use the key to unlock it. Professional handcuffs allow for *double-locking*. They are designed to prevent further tightening once they are double-locked. This helps diminish undue and unintended bruising on those who must wear them. It also makes the cuffs harder to shim open or pick. The key must first be rotated in one direction then the other to completely open the cuffs. The first turn disables the double-locking mechanism;

Handcuff Key

the other direction disengages the ratcheting mechanism and allows one to swivel out of the wrist clasp. Most keys for these types of handcuffs will have a small bit on them that can be used to move a slide, or be inserted in a specific hole to engage the double-lock.

Notice that some of the keys pictured here appear to have more than one bit. This is because many warded locks actually need to have two locking bolts moved at the same time in order to unlock them, such as the example warded padlock in this book.

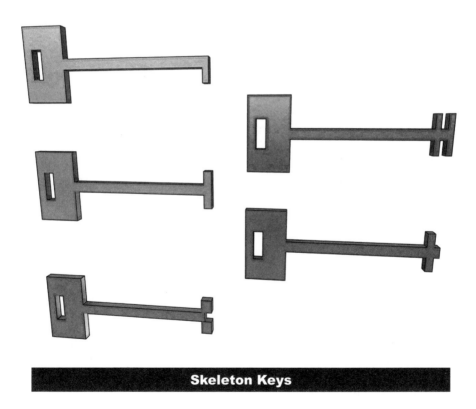

Skeleton Keys

Impressioning Warded Locks

Impressioning warded locks is a method you can use to create a new key for a lock without having the original key, or even knowing its shape. Usually, it is very easy to only use just a skeleton key or L shaped tool to manipulate warded locks open. Sometimes, however, you will find that producing an actual key is useful. To start making your own key, you will first need a suitable *blank*. It may often be difficult to find an actual blank for many warded locks, as they are either uncommon or considered too cheap to bother duplicating. An appropriate blank to start with must fulfill the following requirements:

- Comfortably fit into the key hole, but not so thick as to scrape along the keyway.

- Wide enough to fill the width of the keyway so that it can actually turn or move what is needed to unlock the lock.

- Strong enough to handle a good amount of force without breaking or bending too much.

- Be able to withstand the stresses of grinding, filing, or cutting without cracking or breaking.

A key for a different lock of the same type is often a perfect item with which to start. However, any long flat piece of metal will usually suffice. A jigsaw blade can easily fulfill these requirements. The blades come in a variety of sizes, so hopefully, one will work with your lock. They are also quite cheap and easy to find. Black jigsaw blades are very common, but it may be harder to see marks on it when using the soot approach described

Jigsaw Blade

below. If you choose to work with a jigsaw blade, it is a good idea to grind or file down the teeth of the blade for safety.

As a tool, files work great, are easy to find, and are very inexpensive. A grinding wheel, however, will help your work proceed more quickly and easily. You can find these at most local hardware stores. A thinner cutting wheel will enable you to have more precise cuts than the thick stone wheel which usually comes with the motor. Grinding wheels can be a hassle to transport, however, and thus lack the portability and control that files provide. For both fast and accurate results you can ultimately use a wheel for the majority of your cutting, while using files for the finishing touches.

Blank

Once you have a good starting blank, you are ready to begin impressioning. You will need to put a coating on the blank that can be easily scratched off or marked on. A common method used to achieve this coating is to hold a blank above the flame of a lit candle. The soot that rises in the smoke above the candle will cover the blank with a thin black coating, which can easily be scratched off. At times, however, it may scratch off too easily. If you are working with a black blade, marks may be hard to see, unless you hold it up to the light and look for differences in reflections. Make a few practice scratches to see what they look like. Holding the blade over a gas stove will not work, as there is no smoke or burning residue to leave a coating. Another method is to wait for the candle to melt some wax and then coat the blank with an even layer of wax. You can dip the blank in the molten pool of wax near the flame. Alternatively, you can break off a strip of wax that has dripped down the side of the candle and place it on top of the blade. This can be melted into an even layer by placing the key above the flame. If the wax layer is too thick, it can scratch off when the blank is inserted into the keyway entrance. Practice will help you determine how much to apply. If you would prefer, simply painting the key blank can also work well.

When you are satisfied with your coating, then you can begin the actual task of impressioning. If you can't insert the blank into the lock without scratching the surface, your coating or your blade is too thick. After successfully inserting the blank completely into the lock, rotate it with a good amount of torque in both directions. It should hit the wards inside the

Blank with Marks

lock and not turn very far. Your goal is to have the wards mark the coating on your blank. It helps to jiggle the blank slightly to make the marks more visible.

New Key

Now gently pull out the blade, making certain not to introduce new markings as you do so. You should be able to see grooves and scars made by the wards on the surface of the blade. You simply have to cut away the portions of your blank that have marks on them. Ignore any long marks down the length of the key blank that you made while inserting or removing it. Once you cut away the parts of the blank that get in the way of the wards, your new key should open the lock!

Be careful of certain locks that have a small pin, peg, or obstruction in the lock at the rear of the keyway. Their keys have a tip that is U shaped, hollow, or has a hole at the end. This is needed to work around the rod. When inserted, the key fits around the rod and can rotate without problem. If you cannot observe an *end ward* simply by looking into the keyway, you may have to coat the end of the key to check if there is an end ward in your way.

Some cheap padlocks may require you to push the shackle in and out a bit while turning the key for it to open properly. If it still does not work, repeat the impressioning process. You may not have cut enough, or the wards may be oddly shaped, so that they do not make a full mark at first. Some locks may have wards that only get in the way after you turn the key. These locks will also require you to impression several times. You may have to slide your new key in or out slightly for it to work properly. If you have cut away too much of the key, you can either start over, or you can fill in the cut. Solder works well if the lock does not require too much force. It is soft, though, and will not last very long.

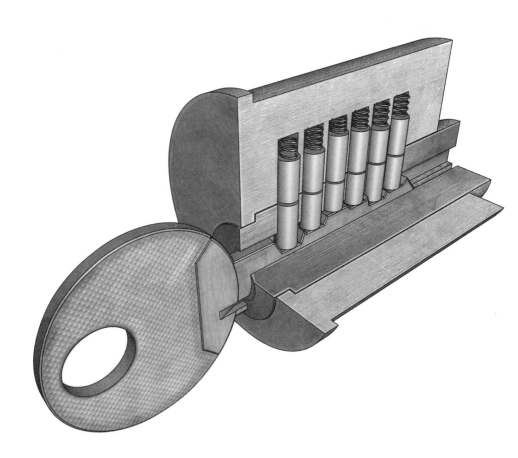

2

Pin
Tumblers

Pin Tumblers

The *pin tumbler* is the most commonly found lock in the United States. It is the meat and potatoes of lock technology. You may be surprised to know it is also one of the oldest lock technologies. Existing since biblical times, a form of the pin tumbler lock with long wooden keys was even found in ancient Egyptian pyramids. In fact, these devices are even older than the fork. Instead of preventing a cylindrical plug from rotating, the Egyptians' lock prevented a large bolt from sliding. These locks lacked springs and top pins, but were very revolutionary for their day. They eventually gave way to other styles of locks and were mostly forgotten. It would take until the mid 1800's for Linus Yale, founder of the Yale Lock Company, to implement the modern pin tumbler with two pins in each pin stack. His son continued his work and created a viable mass-manufactured commercial product by 1865. Today, there is a vast selection of pin tumblers from which to choose. They vary in quality, size, number of possible combinations, and cost, and are essential to providing a sense of security for our society. Whether or not this sense of security is justified, is up to you to decide.

Identifying Pin Tumblers

Pin tumblers can be found in many places, most commonly on house deadbolts, doorknobs, cabinets, padlocks, etc… They usually have *pins* visible in the keyway. These pins are often round and somewhat pointed at the end. The pins are spring-loaded and will spring back down when you push up on them. They look somewhat similar to *wafer tumbler* locks, which will be discussed in a later chapter.

How Pin Tumblers Work

It may take some time to grasp the inner workings of the pin tumbler. So, please don't get discouraged. If you are not completely comfortable with the concept, read this section over again a few times. In addition to the diagrams here, it will help if you actually get a lock and take it apart to see how the internal parts interact with each other. Be careful: there are small parts under spring pressure that will fly all over the room if you are not careful.

Parts of a Pin Tumbler Lock

Although many pin tumbler locks have five pin columns, the number may vary depending on the quality of the lock.

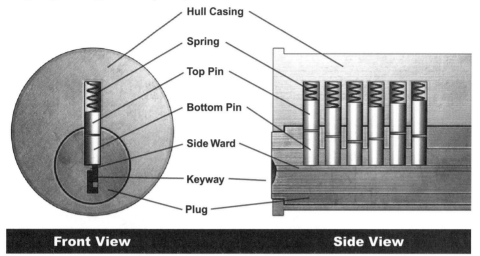

| Front View | Side View |

First, let's become familiar with the components inside the lock:

- The *keyway* is the opening into which the *key* is inserted.

- The side *wards* in the pin tumbler design are lengthwise protrusions along the sides of the keyway. These wards fit into the grooves along the side of the key. They also keep the springs from pushing the pins all the way out.

- The inner cylinder, which rotates as you turn the key, is called the *plug*.

- The *hull,* or *casing,* of the lock is the outer cylinder. This hull remains fixed in place and does not move.

- Each set of pins has a *spring,* which pushes the pins down.

- Each pin column in the lock actually has two pins. One rests on top of the other. Only one is really visible to your eyes, unless you take the lock apart. The *top pin* is dubbed the *driver pin,* because it drives, or pushes, the lower pin down. All of the driver pins are typically of the same size.

- The *bottom pin* of each set is called the *key pin*, since it is the pin that actually makes contact with the key. When the key is not inside the keyway, the key pins often rest on the ward. The key pins vary in length and match up with the notches in the key. They usually have a somewhat pointed end that is visible.

Theory of Operation

Before any key is inserted into the lock, the springs will push the top pins down. These top pins will extend past the hull and into the plug. As these pins protrude into the holes in the plug, they will hold the plug in place and prevent it from rotating. The bottom pin can also stop the plug from turning if it is pushed too far up and is partially inside the lock hull cylinder. As long as there is a pin that crosses the dividing line between the hull and the plug, the cylinder will be locked.

When the correct key is inserted into the lock, the *blade* of the key raises the pins. The bottom pins will rest on the notches of the key. Notice how the size of the notches complements the size of the bottom pins exactly; the longer the bottom pin, the deeper the cut into the key. When the key notch is at the correct height, the separation between the top pin and the bottom pin will be at the same height as the separation between the hull and the plug. This line of separation is called the *shear line*. When this occurs at every *pin column*, there are no longer any pins obstructing the shear line that prevent the plug from rotating. The key can now turn and unlock the lock.

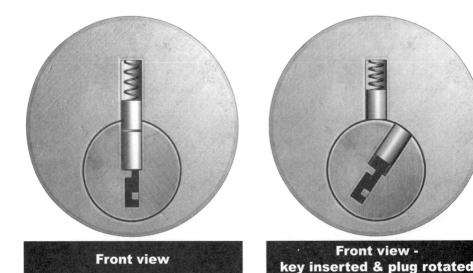

Front view

Front view -
key inserted & plug rotated

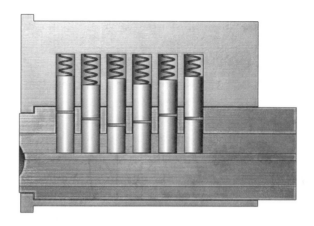

Side view cutaway

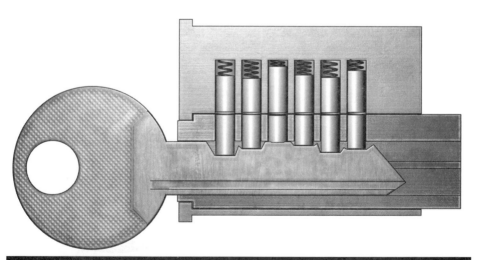

Side view cutaway - key inserted

Standard Tools

There are standard sets of tools that many locksmiths and security professionals use. By no means are you limited to just these professional tools. You can find many common objects that will work just as well, if not better.

The *handle* is that portion of the pick or tool that you hold. Because you make actual contact with this portion, you should be especially careful to find one with which you are completely comfortable. The handles used for most of the picks will probably be the same for all of the picks and rakes in your set. It is critical to find one with a good feel, because the picks and torque wrench are your only form of sensory input that reveal to you what occurs inside the lock.

The *tang* or *stem* of the pick is the long thin metal portion between the tip and the handle. This should be strong enough not to bend excessively; but at the same time, it should be thin enough to be maneuverable in the keyway and not obstruct the pin's movement.

The *tip* should allow for easy insertion, removal, and maneuverability in the keyway. It should also give you a good feel for the pins. This sense of feedback is very crucial to your success.

Don't get too caught up in the memorization of the various rake designs. If for some reason one doesn't work, you can always try another one. Each lock has its own personality; and through experience you will learn which picks work best in which locks.

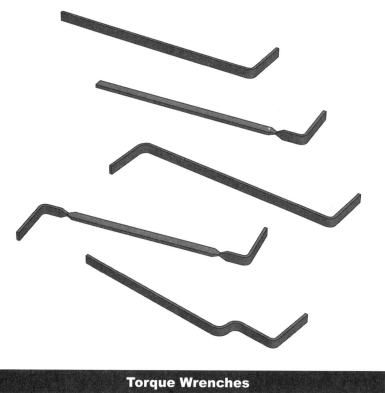

Torque Wrenches

The wrench is a very important tool. Its purpose is not only to turn the plug, but to help you feel what is going on inside the lock. The shorter end is inserted into the keyway, while you push on the longer end to turn the plug. It is important to select the appropriate wrench for the lock you are working with. The torque wrench is used to apply a rotational force on the plug. It is important that the wrench is not too large, so that you will have plenty of room to maneuver your pick in the keyway. Also, it cannot be too small, since it must neither be too weak nor unable to grip the keyway and rotate the plug. Some of these torque wrenches have small springs built into them that give them a bit of play. Some people prefer the softer, more forgiving, spring versions. Others prefer solid ones that allow you to more directly feel the sensations inside the lock. In a pinch, a bent flathead screwdriver may be used as an effective torque wrench.

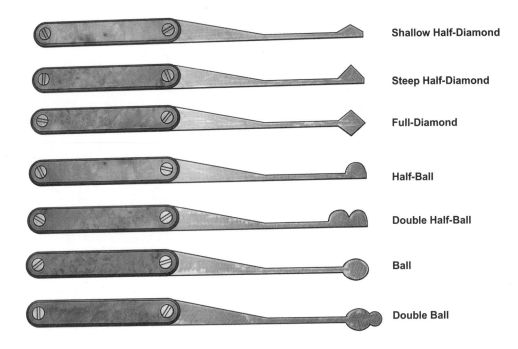

Shallow Half-Diamond

Steep Half-Diamond

Full-Diamond

Half-Ball

Double Half-Ball

Ball

Double Ball

Various Lock Picks / Rakes

Many of the tools listed may be used for various purposes. They may be appropriate for both raking and picking. These are just some suggestions of common uses for these tools. Feel free to use any tool that works in your situation. Jury-rigged and homebrew tools can work just as well, or better, if made properly.

- *Shallow Half-Diamond.* Some advantages of this pick are that it is easy to insert, remove, and rake over the keys both forward and backward. It is good for locks where the key pins are of similar length. If the difference in neighboring pin heights is too great, the diamond won't be able to lift one pin up high enough without lifting its neighbor up too high.

- *Steep Half-Diamond.* This pick is similar to the shallow half-diamond except that it can accommodate greater differences in pin height. Because it is steeper, it is harder to move from pin to pin. You can get half-diamond picks with different *front angles* and *back angles.* Besides picking, diamonds are useful for raking, vibrating, and reverse picking.

- *Full Diamond.* Useful when the lock has pins or wafers on both sides of the keyway.

- *Half-Ball.* Works well for disc tumblers as the ball can roll from wafer to wafer.

- *Double Half-Ball.* Just like a half-ball, but helps with raking wafer locks.

- *Ball.* Useful when the lock has disks on both sides.

- *Double Ball.* Twice the fun.

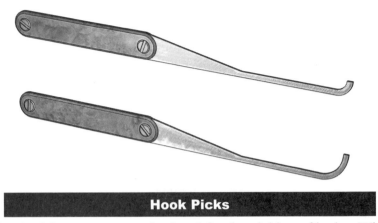

Hook Picks

These hook picks are your standard tool for the picking of locks. With them you can feel each pin individually and lift them without disturbing their neighboring pins.

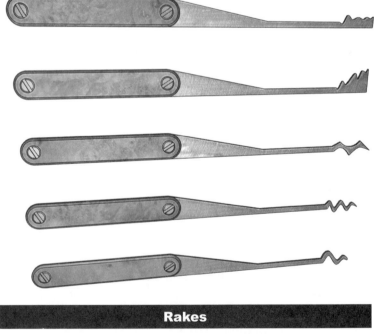

Rakes

Designs for rakes differ greatly. They vary in the number and shape of bumps and grooves. Some vaguely resemble keys, while others look almost seemingly random. Various bumps, grooves, ridges, and protrusions are designed to mimic keys. Raking with these tools can cause several pins at once to bounce across the shear line.

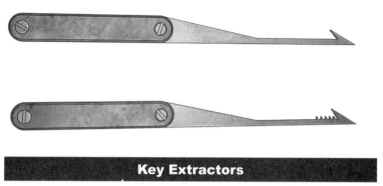

Key Extractors

As the name implies, the key extractor is used to remove broken key segments that are still stuck in the lock's keyway. Extractors are usually hook shaped, or have one-way teeth that allow it to be inserted easily, but then can grip and pull out the obstructing object.

Curved Ball Pick

Sometimes it helps to have an extra curve or odd shape to the pick to match the size or shape of the lock. As you deal with locks of various sizes you should build up a collection of different pick styles.

Keyless Entry

Keep in mind that even if you read this book and fully understand the operation of a pin tumbler lock you may still be completely unable to pick them on your first attempt. There is no substitute for practice. Get yourself some locks of varying qualities in order to experiment. You will also need a set of picks with which to work. If you need, you can even make your own. The easiest way, by far, to get picks is to purchase a set from a security supply company or other distributor.

In order to successfully *pick* the pin tumbler, all you really need is a torque wrench and a hook pick. There are many other ways, though, to unlock a pin tumbler. Picking a lock is the standard and most versatile method. Since *raking* is easier and quicker, it is often a much more suitable solution than normal picking. For greater speed, you can also use an automatic picking tool. Don't forget that you can often bypass the lock entirely.

You have probably seen many movies where an actor will pick a lock with some random household object, or even an authentic lock pick. Usually, the actor will use only one tool: the pick. The general populace, therefore, readily believes that a lock can be opened with just one tool. This is generally not the case. Most methods of picking require the simultaneous use of two tools: one to turn the plug, and the other to pick the pins. The tool that applies a rotational force is called the *torque wrench*. You can use any object that can be inserted in the keyway to rotate it. The second tool is usually a *pick* or *rake* that is used to manipulate the pins. In a normal pin tumbler, it would be difficult for the same tool to manipulate pins, while also turning the cylinder.

Locks kept outside and exposed to the elements can become quite dirty. Locations with lots of grease or dirt can also get the lock cylinder dirty and clogged. This can make picking the lock much more difficult. You may find that it helps to clean out the lock before you attempt to pick it. White gasoline or electronic spray cleaner can work well for this purpose. It will also help with the normal operation of the lock.

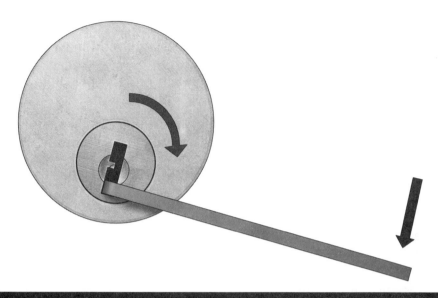

Placement of Torque Wrench in keyway

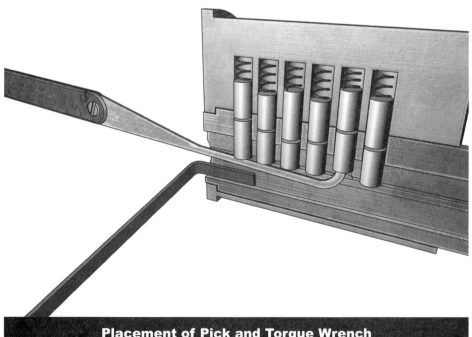

**Placement of Pick and Torque Wrench
in lock keyway for picking**

Raking

Raking is a much easier skill to learn than picking. But while it is easy to learn, it is difficult to master. Raking requires the locksmith to have just the right "touch." This is something that can only be learned through practice, practice, and more practice. An advantage of the raking method is that it can be one of the fastest hand methods employed. It also works on both pin tumblers and wafer locks, which will be covered in a later chapter.

The idea is to simply take a raking pick and repetitively pull it across all the pins in such a fashion that it unlocks the lock. While this may sound too simple, it can work if done properly.

First, place a torque wrench into the lower portion of the keyway. Make sure there is plenty of room left to maneuver the pick around the pins. Now, apply a **gentle** amount of turning force on the wrench in the direction that the key would turn when unlocking the lock. It is critical that you apply an appropriate amount of force. Usually, the amount of force applied is much less than what you might imagine. The force used to push up on the pins can be much greater than that used on the wrench. Only a slight amount is usually needed. As frustration sets in, people have a tendency to apply too much force. This will only lead to more frustration. Take a break. Let what you learned sink in and try again when you are refreshed. Try allotting 15 minutes or so at a time. Afterward, concentrate on what you felt and compare it to what you were expecting to feel. It is important to get a good feel for the lock. Understand its personality and how it reacts to your actions. Remember, take your time and get in sync with the lock. Do not try to rush the process.

Now, while you are applying this slight force on the torque wrench, put the raking pick all the way to the rear of the keyway. Apply a gentle force up and into the last pin. Now, remove the rake while continuing to apply a slight, constant force on all of the pins. Try to keep the force constant to all of the pins, even though your position might have to change and the feedback from each pin will be different. Make certain you give each pin a chance; don't skip over any, especially the first pin.

Your first pass will most likely not be successful, so give it a good number of passes. With each pass of the pick, slightly increase the amount of force on the torque wrench. Remember, though, you should still not rotate with too much force. After going back and forth a good number of times, you can try a different style of rake. After a while with no success, you may need to release all pressure on the wrench to let all the pins drop. If one of the pins is pushed up too far and the bottom pin is binding in place, it may be best to just start all over again.

Many people will hold the pick as they would a pen. They are comfortable with this and can very easily control where the end of the pick is located and how much force is applied. With some raking techniques, however, a different hold is useful. Try holding the rake at its center of mass with only two fingers. This acts like a pivot point. You can use your other fingers to limit the amount of up and down movement that the rake is allowed to swivel. For more control over the force being applied with the rake, use a finger to push down on the back of the handle. This will push the tip of the rake up and into the pins. Now, you can control the forward and backward motion with two fingers and the force being applied with a third.

Some locks prefer a quick light stroke to jostle the pins into place. With two fingers holding the center of the rake, you can control how much the rake moves in and out, as well as vibrate the rake up and down. Rapidly move the rake forward and backward inside the keyway. Or, when your rake is inside the keyway, start making quick up and down movements. Do this quickly and vigorously, but not too hard. Vary the force you apply to the pins and to the torque wrench. This gives the pins a chance to set. Try not to allow the pins to get stuck up too high. You will notice that the vertical movement of the pin is less than the vertical movement you apply to the rake. Try to emulate a hummingbird with a soft touch at high speed. Maintain a loose hold on the rake, as you accelerate the rake up and down. You will find that cheaper locks are especially susceptible to this style of raking. Keep in mind that this quick method does not work very well with better locks.

Different rakes and styles of raking work better for different styles of locks. Experience and practice will show you which ones work better. Locks that have all of the pins of a similar length will rake much easier. Some locks will be very unyielding to raking. You may have to pick these locks or use a combination of raking and picking. Get a variety of locks in your collection, so that you can be comfortable with a variety of locks and techniques.

Picking

Picking is a technique whereby you try to *set* each of the pins individually. This method can be used on both pin tumblers and wafer tumblers. You have to know more about the inner workings of the lock to pick it, but the knowledge will help you greatly when you later attempt other methods. Your goal, when picking, is to clear the shear line and make certain that there are no pins obstructing it.

The Concept

If locks were perfectly manufactured, it would be impossible to pick each individual pin. But in the real world, locks have various imperfections and are built to a certain set of machining tolerances. The higher the quality of the lock, the tighter the tolerances, and the harder it is to pick. Numerous pieces of metal have to slide, rotate, and move close to each other. Because of this, there must be slight gaps to allow for this motion. It is important to remember that this makes picking locks possible.

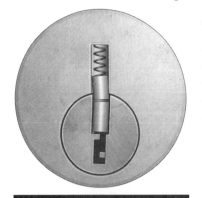

Top Pin Binding

The first aspect we are going to look at is an important effect called *binding*. Binding occurs when a rotational force is applied to the plug, while you try to rotate the cylinder with your torque wrench. The plug and the hull essentially crimp the top pin, holding it in place. The hull remains fixed in place. When you turn the plug, the hull and plug grab the pin.

The ability to pick individual pins occurs when locks are made with small imperfections in manufacturing, sometimes as small as .0002 inches. The holes drilled for the pin columns will not lie exactly in a straight line that is exactly parallel with the axis of revolution of the plug. Because of this, when you rotate the plug, it will only bind one or a few pins at first. The others will remain loose and will still be able to move up and down more freely. Each lock is built with its own characteristics and will have its own order in which the pins set. Remember, the order in which the pins set will be reversed, depending on which direction you attempt to turn the plug. Also, note that metal is somewhat elastic. If you turn too hard on the torque wrench, the pins will "give" slightly; and more of them will bind. In order to avoid this situation, make certain that you don't apply too much force on your torque wrench.

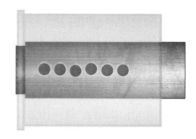

First, use your pick to determine which pin is binding, or being held in place, the most. You can now use your pick to push up on that pin. As you push up on the bottom pin, it will, in turn, push up on the top pin, until

Pin Column Misalignment

you get to the point where the top pin is completely inside the hull and past the shear line. The plug, that before was crimping the top pin, all of a sudden now has nothing in its way to keep it from rotating. Since you are still applying a light rotational force, the plug will start and continue to rotate, until it hits the next top pin and stops again. Because of the extra rotation, the hole in the plug and the hole in the hull of the first pin now no longer exactly line up. The spring can push down on the top pin all it wants, but the pin will catch on the edge of the plug and stay completely lodged in the hull. It is now trapped. When this happens, the pin is *set*. Neither the top pin nor the bottom pin is obstructing the shear line. This is the goal we are attempting to achieve.

Pin has been set

Now, simply repeat this process for the rest of the pins. When you set the last pin the plug will be free to rotate and you will have unlocked it. Congratulations!

When you are pushing up on the pins, you have to be finely tuned to feel just the right point when they set. Make certain to stop after the pin is set. If you continue applying upward pressure on the pin and keep pushing it up further, then you can

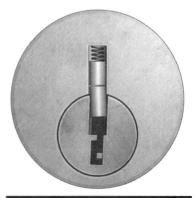

Bottom Pin Binding

force the bottom pin up into the hull as well. The rotational force on the plug will now bind the bottom pin instead of the top pin. They will both be stuck up in the hull, and the bottom pin will keep the plug from rotating. You can tell if this is happening when you remove your pick from the pin, and the bottom pin refuses to fall down. This is also not good because the bottom pin is now blocking the shear line and will prevent further pins from binding properly. It will also keep the lock from opening.

You have properly set the pin if you remove the pick from the bottom pin; and it falls down freely, without the spring pushing it down. At this point, another pin should be binding; and the whole process can be repeated. If you set the pins toward the front of the lock first, and they have long lower pins, then they may act as an obstacle for your picking tool to work behind them. If there is a short lower pin between two long pins, it may also be a problem. A good hook pick is designed to curve around these obstacles and allows you to manipulate the pins you want and avoid the ones you don't.

Bottom Pin Falls Freely

Your Turn

Now it's your turn to start picking pin tumblers. First, insert a pick and torque wrench into the keyway. Apply a **gentle** turning pressure with the turning tool. Again, the word "gentle" is emphasized. If too many pins bind, it will jam the lock. If the pins that do bind are too difficult to push up, then you are also turning too hard. When you become frustrated and tired, you will likely start turning harder. When this happens, take a break and recover. Well-machined locks, and those made to tighter tolerances, will require the use of more torque. Padlocks and some doorknobs also have to turn a spring-loaded locking bolt, so these require more torque. Experience will tell you how much to apply. When you pick padlocks, there is the additional skill of holding the lock in the same hand that you use to turn the wrench. With practice, you will learn the method that suits you best. Try a variety of methods. Remember, this isn't always an exact science.

While you are applying this gentle turning pressure, use the pick to feel the pins. Don't use your sight. Just feel them. By knowing how they respond in various situations, you can create an internal map in your mind of what the lock looks like and the state of all the pins. Remember to visualize. This is a critical skill to learn. Just as many athletes try to visualize before a game what they will have to perform, so should you visualize yourself and how you will pick the lock before you attempt it.

Next, attempt to determine which pin is binding the most. Then position your pick directly under it and use the tip of your pick to make contact with the bottom of the pin. Apply a small amount of force, pushing the pin upward in your attempt to push the top pin completely into the upper chamber of the lock. Be certain not to disturb the neighboring pins too much during this process. There are a variety of hook pick sizes that are better for different shaped locks. Also, you can use any other type of pick or rake that works well for you. Remember, the only rule is to use what works.

When the top pin completely clears the shear line and enters the hull, you will have set the pin. This is also called *breaking* the pin. When this happens, you will hear or feel a small click. When your senses are in tune with this, it will become an earth-shattering event. You will feel the pin respond differently. At first, you had to fight against both the top pin binding and the spring pushing down. For a brief moment in the gap, there will be just the spring resisting you. Then, there will be a large resistance as the bottom pin hits the edge of the hole in the hull. You must get used to how this feels. You will also feel the click in the hand that is holding the torque wrench. The wrench will give and the plug will rotate ever so slightly, and then stop. Although you can feel this, you probably won't be able to see it. Treat the tools as extensions of your body. Don't trust your eyes; use your other senses to experience the lock.

After you have broken the pin, lower your pick and make sure that the bottom key pin also falls freely down. If it stays up, then you have pushed the pin up too far. You can choose either to relieve some tension from the wrench in order to let it drop, or start over. If the spring pushes the pin down, then you haven't set it. Perhaps this pin isn't the one binding the most, you didn't push up far enough, or you didn't apply enough force to the wrench.

The next step is to move on to the next pin. Feel the remaining pins that have not broken and try to determine the next one that is binding the most. This will be your next target. Repeat the steps listed above with that pin. If you set a pin and other pins fall, or if you are unable to set any more pins, you may have set one in the wrong order. Clear the lock by releasing all pressure on the wrench and start over again.

When the last pin is set, the shear line will be clear with no obstructions and the plug will be free to rotate. The lock is now open! The actual mechanics behind each lock that unlocks, frees, or opens vary even more drastically than the locks themselves. Padlocks usually have to actuate a spring-loaded locking bolt in order to release the shackle. This means that you need to apply a little more torque. It also means that when they do open the lock, it will jump somewhat. This can be a very satisfying feeling.

Since all locks are different and the holes are off axis in a different order, the pins of each lock set in a different order. This is entirely due to the tolerances with which they are made. The cheaper the lock, the more the holes are off axis; and the easier the pins are to set.

Always remember to return the lock to either a locked or unlocked position. If you leave it in an intermediate position, the key may not be able to be inserted in the keyway. This is because the pins are unable to *float,* or move up into the hull, and get out of the way of the incoming key. It is this same concept that prevents you from removing the key while it is in an intermediate position. It is also easy to return the plug to either the locked or unlocked position. As long as it is in an intermediate position, the plug is free spinning. Be sure the top pins don't get stuck in the keyway if you turn the plug completely upside down.

Alternative Method

There is an alternative method of picking if you wish to think less and speed things up a bit. Start in the rear of the lock by trying to pick the last pin. If it doesn't set, just move on to the next pin. Go through each of the pins and try to set them all from back to front. In reality, only one or two will probably set. Just go back and start at the rear of the lock and do all of the ones that haven't yet set. With each pass over the pins one or two will set. Eventually, all of the pins will set; and the lock will open. The advantage of this method is that you do not have to pay as much attention to each individual pin. It is a good idea to slightly increase the torque you are applying with each pass you make over the pins. This method is used for speed, but it may not work as well with high security locks that have modified pins designed to false set.

Wrap Up

Also, keep in mind that the reaction of the pins will be different if the lock is "upside-down;" that is, the pins are on the bottom of the keyway rather than the top. The main difference is that the pins that are set will stay down instead of free-falling back down into the keyway. Some people find this easier to deal with. Only the pins that have not yet set will be sticking into the keyway. If you are picking a padlock, then you will also have to deal with holding the lock itself. You can hold the padlock any way you want and will soon find a way that is comfortable for you. Try to hold the lock and the tension wrench with the same hand. Some locks also have pins in the sides or the bottom of the keyway. The general picking concept is basically the same. You will just have to adjust for the new locations of the pins.

The knowledge you have gained by reading the material so far is more than enough to pick almost all common pin tumbler locks. There are other important aspects that are useful to know: master keys, plug size variations, beveling, spacer pins, false sets, modified pins, angled cams, plug spinners, and mushroom pins, some of which are concepts that will be covered in the advanced pin tumblers chapter. But don't rush into these concepts. First, take a break and absorb the newly learned material. Don't try to learn everything at once. Make certain that you are comfortable with picking a wide variety of locks.

It is important that you have a clear understanding of what you are doing in order to be able to do it again. Later on, when you move to higher security locks, you will probably have to refine some of what you are used to doing. At the beginning, it is best not to overwhelm yourself. Begin with a very cheap lock. Cheap locks are usually made to much looser tolerances and are much easier to pick. When you are ready, move on to progressively harder and harder locks. Practicing on a wide variety of locks will give you a wider range of experiences. This will allow you to adapt to new and stranger locks much faster.

Exercises

Understanding how the lock responds is very important. When you first attempt to open a lock, the pins will do their own thing and the lock may open even if you do not recognize exactly when the various pins set. Or, you may not be sure exactly when you push the bottom pins up into the hull. In order for you to get the right feel to know what the pins are doing, here are a few exercises you can try.

First, find or buy a practice lock. These can be bought from almost any hardware store or locksmith. If you want to practice with pin tumblers, be sure to get a pin tumbler. When you are first learning, make certain that it is one that is relatively easy to pick. Usually, you can use price as a guideline for its difficulty. Lower priced locks are a lot easier to pick. Locks designated for deadbolts make good choices for this exercise purpose. Feel free to pick up a more difficult lock for practicing on later, or for making comparisons.

Now, open the lock and remove the plug. Be careful when you do this, as the springs and pins will fly out. It will help to use a *plug follower*. A plug follower is a tool that you can use to push the plug out of the lock. It should be about the same size as the actual plug so that it can keep the spring loaded top pins safely in the outer hull. Make-shift wooden dowel rods or thick pens are often used for this purpose. A trick you can do is cut a strip of plastic from a two-liter bottle and roll it in a tight roll. As you push this into the lock in place of the plug, it can expand to fill the hole and keep the top pins in place. Since it is transparent, it also gives you a chance to better see what the pins and holes look like while you are learning.

The key will only work the lock if the bottom pins are in the correct order. If you want to use the key again in the future, be certain to take note of the order of the key pins. Of course, what do you really need the key for? At this point, reassemble the lock, but with only one pin. Remove the top pins and springs from the other pin stacks. Picking this lock should now be very easy. Push up on the single pin with a hook pick, while applying a rotational torque with a torque wrench. When it reaches the breaking point, the plug will spin. Feel how the key pin is binding and the plug holds it in place. Also, feel how you can almost sense when the plug will turn a split-second before it actually does.

Take the lock apart again. Now, put it back together, only this time with two pins. While applying a small amount of torque, first push up on the front pin, then the back pin. Notice how one of them binds and the other one is springy. If they are both binding, then you know you are applying too much force. This is a very valuable lesson.

Now that you know how to determine which pin is binding, push up on that pin until you feel it "set." Become familiar with this feeling. Set the pin, clear it, and then set it again a few times. This is the response that you are trying to detect when you pick locks. After you set it, notice how the bottom pin free falls down. Feel how the pin is now loose in its pin column and is neither binding in place nor has the spring pushing down on it. Now, set the pin and continue to push up. There will be significant resistance, and then the bottom pin will begin to enter the hull. When this occurs, the bottom pin will bind and the resistance of the pin will be as it was when it was the top pin that was binding. That is why it is so important that you are familiar with the feeling of a pin setting. If you do not notice it, you might keep pushing the pin up and the bottom pin will bind and get stuck in the hull. You can tell if this has happened when you remove your pick and the bottom pin remains up in the hull. It neither free-falls down nor is it being pushed down by the spring. Experiment with this for a while and become familiar with it.

Set the first pin that binds and make certain that the bottom pin falls. Move your pick to the second pin and notice how it is now binding. Compare this to how it was springy before. You should be able to push up on the second pin, and as soon as you hit the breaking point, the plug will rotate. The last pin is always the most fun.

Repeat this process by progressively adding pins back into the lock one by one, until you are comfortable with picking the lock with all pins. Feel free to intersperse this with the more difficult lock(s) that you obtained. Also, make sure to interlace this exercise with frequent breaks. When something works well, stop and concentrate on what you did to make it work. Focus on that and try to repeat it again. Eventually, you will be quite comfortable with more types of locks.

To make things easier, use your *plug follower*. This is a valuable tool for locksmiths. Instead of taking the lock apart in a bag or box to catch the flying springs, you simply unlock the lock and place the plug follower on the face of the plug and push. The plug follower is exactly the same diameter as the plug and will hold the driver pins and springs in the hull. The plug will just have the bottom pins inside, which you can move around to *re-key* the lock. When you are done re-keying, take the plug and push the plug follower out with it. By doing this, the driver pins and springs never leave the lock and never have a chance to get lost. To perform these exercises, though, you will have to remove the top pins and springs. Try not to lose these small pieces.

Plug Follower

When practicing with pin tumbler locks, it often helps to remove some pins from the pin stack to make them easier to pick when learning. Or, you might be trying to follow the exercises in this book. Or, maybe you just want to see what the pins look like for yourself. Sometimes the pins and springs are inserted from the top of the lock, which is then covered with a metal strip. At other times, it may be simpler to remove the plug in order to see what is inside the lock. If you want to easily see the inside of your lock, without damaging it or losing small pieces, you should follow a few simple steps. Having a plug follower is critical to performing this task. If you simply pushed the plug out or the hull, then all the top pins could fall into the void left by the plug, and springs can fly everywhere or be stuck sticking out of the hull. You need to follow the plug with another object that will keep the top pins and springs inside the hull. An object that would work well might be a glass cylinder that matches the size of the plug. This would hold the pins and springs in place while still allowing you to see the lock internals. However, obtaining such a cylinder for just viewing that one lock size could be a waste of your time and money. A dowel rod would also work, except that you can't see through it, and it would still have to be specifically matched to each lock size. Instead, you can create a versatile plug follower with a two-liter plastic soda bottle and scissors. Simply cut out a rectangular piece of plastic from the side of a translucent soda bottle.

Then, roll up the rectangle into a cylinder that matches the cylindrical shape of the plug. The cylinder will have a tendency to unroll, and this is a good thing. Once the cylinder is inside the hull, it will unroll to exactly match the size of the plug. You may want to use some tape to help you keep the cylinder rolled up before you start pushing the cylinder with it. Be prepared to remove the tape once the plastic cylinder is inserted into the hull.

Plastic Plug Follower

Before you can just push the plug out of the lock you may need to prepare it for removal. First, pick the lock or insert the key into the plug so that all of the pins will align with the shear line. None of the pins will hold the plug in place, but there is usually some other mechanical piece preventing you from pulling out the plug with your key. Take a look at the back of the plug. There might be a small, metal piece attached to it that prevents it from sliding out of the hull. This metal holder can often be removed by unscrewing, or with the aid of a pair of pliers. As you remove the holder, make sure not to pull or push out the plug accidentally. Line up the rolled up plastic cylinder behind the plug and start pushing the plastic cylinder into the hull which pushes the plug out of the hull.

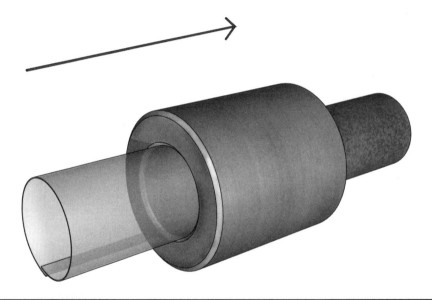

Plug Removal

When the plastic roll is all the way in, it will unwind completely and you will be able to see the top pins pressing down on top of the plastic cylinder. Make sure that the bottom pins don't slip out of the plug when the plug is completely removed. When you have satisfied your curiosity or made any desired modifications, you can simply push the plug back in and the plastic roll will slide out. After putting the holder back in its place, the lock should work again.

Bypass Picking

Sometimes you don't have to pick the lock at all in order to open it. You can sometimes merely "bypass" it. This is called *bypass picking*. It takes less skill than actual picking, but requires that the lock allows for it. This method only works on lighter security locks that have an exposed locking bolt in the rear of the keyway. Many desks, cabinets, and a few padlocks are like this. The concept is simple. Insert your bypass pick all the way into the lock and ignore the pins or wafers completely. Attempt to move the locking bolt manually with your tool. The rear of the plug may have a *tailpiece* that will turn a locking bolt or move some other piece to open the lock. Whatever that tailpiece would have done, you should try to do the same thing to the bolt. You may be able to move it out of the shackle or slot, and allow the lock to open. It is a simple concept, when you are lucky enough to have a lock on which it works.

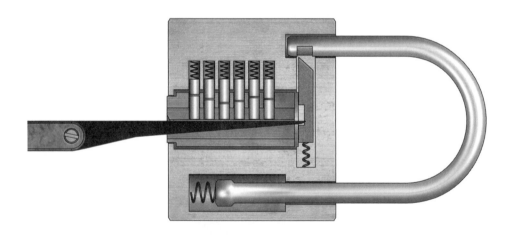

Padlock - Bypass Picking

Other parts of the system may also be actuated, moved, provoked, or manipulated to open the lock. Remember, the lock itself can often be avoided entirely. Be creative and think about what you are trying to accomplish before you jump in and start picking. For example, many cars can simply be opened by sticking a tool down inside the door through the opening for the side window and lifting a bar in the locking assembly. A "Slim Jim" is used for this purpose. A locksmith or other public service official should be very careful when performing this operation, as modern cars contain a plethora of sensitive electronics and wires within their doors. Be very careful not to break anything. Newer models also contain guards that prevent direct access to the locking mechanism. Each make and model of car may require a different and odd-shaped rod in order to reach what you need. Always first consult a manual for the particular make and model of car to determine if it is safe and the appropriate approach to use.

Car Door Shimming Tools

Shimming

Shimming is similar to bypassing, except that you are bypassing the locking bolt from outside the lock instead of from inside the lock. The idea is to insert some sort of object into the locking mechanism and move the locking bolt, or whatever is holding the *shackle* inside the lock, out of the way. Since the mechanisms vary greatly, there is no standard

Padlock Shimming

method for shimming a lock. Here are some examples, though.

Shimming can be very effective on a wide variety of padlocks. Padlocks usually work by having a spring-loaded locking bolt fit into a notch in the shackle in order to hold it inside the lock. Often, the locking bolt will have an angled top, which allows the shackle to be locked without unlocking the lock. This means that the locking bolt must be spring-loaded. So, if you can fit a very thin strong object into the lock parallel to the shackle, you can sometimes slide the locking bolt out of the way and spring the shackle open. This requires that the lock's hole for the shackle is large enough to also allow for the shimming tool to fit inside. This method will also work for warded padlocks. The actual lock type is almost irrelevant. Since many padlocks lock both sides of the latch, you may need to shim both sides simultaneously.

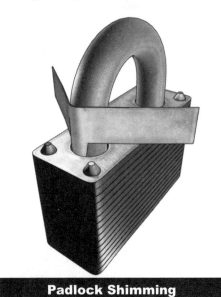

Padlock Shimming

Padlock shims are often sold that are specifically made to help you deal with padlocks with less hassle. They are made of thin yet strong material that can be inserted into the padlock and then rotated to release the latch. They are often tapered to make them much easier to work with.

Padlock Shims

Shimming is also very effective on common doorknobs. The *latch* is the portion of the locking bolt mechanism that sticks out of the door, into the doorjam, and holds the door shut. One side of the latch is angled so that the door can be closed without turning the handle. The door can also be closed while the handle lock is locked. This is because it is spring-loaded. All you need to do is take a tool and stick it in the gap between the doorjam and the door. You may have heard about credit cards being used for this. Try not to break your card if you attempt to use it for this purpose. Most latches will have springs that are too strong and will require a stronger, differently shaped, or better tool for this purpose. Make contact with the bolt and work it back into the door, and the door will open. Although it is difficult, if you can't make contact with the angled side of the latch, you may still be able to use the tool to slowly work the latch back into the door. Some doorjams are better than others at blocking access to the door's latch. Many sophisticated doorknob assemblies used in commercial applications are not susceptible to this. They have additional protrusions that stick out of the door. This *antipick latch* is pushed into the door when the door is closed. The mechanism then mechanically prevents the main latch from being pushed back into the door without opening the lock.

Shimming usually works anytime you have an angled spring-loaded locking bolt. This is why deadbolts are generally much more desirable. They cannot effectively be shimmed, since they are not spring-loaded and cannot simply be pushed back into the door.

Impact and Vibration Picking

When done properly, *impact picking* and *vibration picking* can be one of the fastest ways to open a lock. These methods are also beneficial because they do not require a great amount of skill. These methods work on most pin tumblers, but are less successful with wafer locks and not recommended. Law enforcement officers, or other professionals, who must open locks in emergencies when time is critical, will many times use this method. Often they also have other issues to worry about and do not have the time or inclination to learn the art of lock picking. More automatic picking tools are useful, because they do not require an excessive amount of practicing time. Instead, you can generally pick up the right tool and use it effectively after some experimentation. Experience is still very important for you to have the right touch. These methods also require a lock that is susceptible to this bypass method.

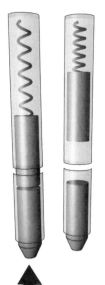

There are really two methods you can use. The first concept is simple. A tool with a rake pick rapidly oscillates over the pins. This movement causes the pins to be violently vibrated up and down with the hope that at some point the shear line will be clear and the plug may rotate. An appropriate amount of torque is applied while the pins are vibrating to catch them as they set. This style of picking acts as an extension of the high-speed, manual racking method. A mechanical system can move faster and more predictably. This makes it more useful in some situations, though less able to adapt to a variety of locks.

The second method uses a snapping motion. A flat tool accelerates towards the pins and strikes them all simultaneously. The physics is similar to billiard balls or those desk toys that have one marble swing and hit a second. The momentum from the first ball is completely absorbed and passed to the second, which moves on with roughly the same speed, leaving the first ball in place. This is what the impact attempts to do. It impacts the tips of the bottom pins with just enough force to knock them into the top pins, thus knocking the top pins up into the hull. The lower pins themselves stay down, because they transfered all of their energy into the top pins.

You really don't have to know all of this theory to effectively use a vibration or impact tool. Just put it in the keyway, pull the trigger, and rotate your torque wrench at just the right time. You must be sure to make contact with each of the pins. When using an impact tool, make certain that you impact the center of each of the pins exactly straight on and at the same time. This means the blade must be exactly parallel to the keyway. Some tools have angled blades to allow holding the tool at an angle if space is tight. These will require a bit more practice to insure that the blade is always parallel and strikes all pins simultaneously. Different locks will require a different amount of force for their pins to bounce properly. The locks must also be in good working order. If the lock is dirty, the pins may be unable to bounce freely inside their chambers.

You do need to have an appropriate *pick gun.* This is a tool you hold in one hand that usually has a lever or trigger that you squeeze with your fingers to provide a vibrating action. Some require that you squeeze and then release to provide the snapping action. Remember, that you still need to use a torque wrench with these devices. Place the pick gun all the way into the keyway, insert the torque wrench, apply a rotating pressure on the wrench and squeeze the trigger. Do not move the gun vertically or laterally while picking. As the pick strikes the pins and knocks them upward, use your torque wrench to cause the plug to catch the top pins as they jump into the hull casing. Most quality pick guns allow you to adjust the force of the snapping action to accommodate different types of locks.

Pick Gun

Snap guns are relatively easy to construct from an appropriate stiff wire. If you are feeling creative,or desperate, ad-hoc versions are possible. These could be made from modified coat hangers, clothespins, or anything that has a springing or vibrating action. Use your imagination in making your new automatic pick tool, or just buy one off the shelf. Some will vibrate the pins

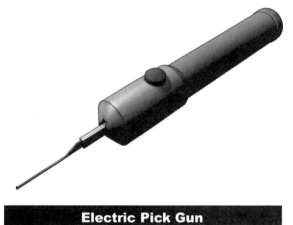

Electric Pick Gun

while others will attempt to snap all of the pins up simultaneously. Modern electric vibrating tools that are battery-powered are also available. It is often believed, however, that electric tools are slightly less effective and more cumbersome. This can depend on your personal style and ability.

A key blank may even be cut with the deepest cuts possible except for small ridges or ramps left on the key blank. This type of key is often called a *999 key, rapping key, bump key, or, bounce key.* The key is placed in the lock so that one ridge is touching each of the pins. This key is then quickly inserted the rest of the way very rapidly and forcefully. As soon as the key is completely inside, it must be rotated. This has to happen quickly enough so that the upper pins do not get a chance to spring back down again. A mallet, screwdriver, or other tool is often used to knock the key into place. This action will, hopefully, bounce all of the pins up and to the shear line. Again, it is important that each of the ramps impact each of the pins at the same time.

Bounce Key

Unfortunately, if the lock is not susceptible to vibration or impact picking, you are out of luck and will have to resort to one of the other previous methods described in this book. Sometimes, though, impact picking is preferred. This is often the case with serrated pins, which you will learn more about in the next chapter.

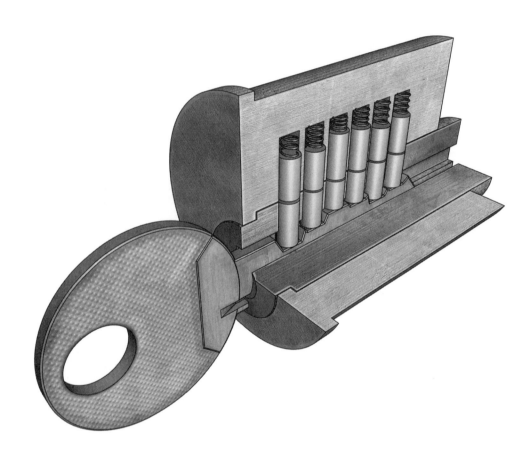

3

Advanced
Pin
Tumblers

Advanced Pin Tumblers

Locks are a constantly evolving technology. Manufacturers are always looking to get a competitive edge by increasing the security of the locks they sell. At the same time, they are also looking to make a profit. Which means they are also trying to make locks as cheaply as possible. Most consumers are not overly obsessed with security and usually consider one lock to be as good as the next. That's why price becomes a deciding factor. Because of this, most of the locks you will find will be relatively inexpensive and easy to pick.

This is not always the case. For those who are looking for more security, there is a wide variety of higher security locks from which to choose. While it may be easy to learn how to pick cheap locks, it can be very difficult to learn how to master high quality, high security locks. Learning to pick higher security locks is a far more challenging task that will demand a greater amount of your time. Advanced lock picking is an art that takes time and talent to develop. You must be in tune with yourself and the lock. Your fingers must be sensitive to minute vibrations and be able to sense more precisely the events that transpire within the lock.

More expensive locks are made to much higher tolerances. This means you have less room for error and must be less sloppy in your work. There will be less play in the plug, it will be harder to bind pins, it will be harder to determine the order that the pins bind, and you must move the pins to a more exact height for them to set. But, there is more. The lock manufacturer may also try to "trick" you. They can make pins that fool you into thinking they have set, when in reality they are still binding and will continue to hold the plug securely in place. Or the manufacturer may place a *dead pin* in place of a normal one. Such a pin is solid and held in place. It is not spring-loaded and will not move up and down. They are used to prevent incorrect keys and picking tools from being used.

This chapter will cover several modifications to traditional pin tumbler locks that manufacturers make in order to increase their security, as well as several techniques you can use to help you pick them more effectively.

Rounded and Beveled

If you peer into the keyway of a pin tumbler, you will probably notice that the bottom end of the bottom pins are somewhat rounded. This allows them to slide up and down with the ramps on the key as it is inserted and removed. If they were not rounded on the bottom, then the flat edge could get stuck on the key and make it difficult for the key to slide in and out.

The ends of the pins that meet the shear line are different. They are normally flat or curved slightly to allow for turning of the plug. The tighter the tolerances, the more exactly the key must lift the pin to precisely the correct height. Sometimes, this is not the case. The manufacturer can also round the ends of the pin that meet at the shear line. The entrances to the holes in the plug and the hull can also be beveled. Rounding and beveling allows for cheaper materials to be used and reduces the tolerances of the key needed to open the lock. When both of these methods are employed, the pins can be slightly at the wrong height and still slide into place when rotating the plug. Besides reducing the tolerances needed, these methods can also extend the useful lifetime of the lock, both of which reduce the cost of making and maintaining these locks.

With cheap locks, both sides of the pins are rounded and both holes are beveled. This can make raking the lock much easier, as there is much more leeway and flexibility on how you move the pins. These angles and curves can pose some problems when picking. The pins can catch on the bevel, or the rounded pin can catch on the edge of the hole. If this pin is held in place, this behaviour can mimic the pin setting. Because the pin isn't at the right height, it can still prevent the plug from rotating. If you find a cheap lock that seems very easy to pick, and the plug turns a bit, but not enough to open, you may be dealing with rounded pins and beveled holes. Loosen your

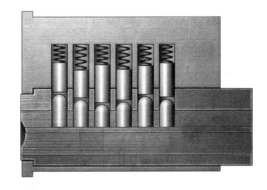

Rounded Lower Pins

torque slightly and try to jiggle the pins into place. Consider using the high speed raking technique if it is a cheap lock. Many low quality devices can be consistently opened in under a second if you use the right feel.

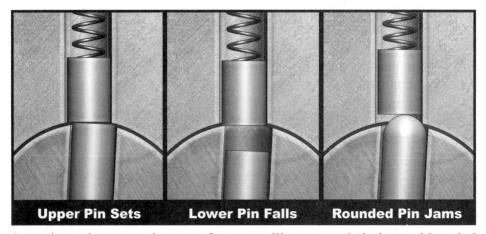

Upper Pin Sets   **Lower Pin Falls**   **Rounded Pin Jams**

Sometimes, however, the manufacturer will use rounded pins and beveled holes to their advantage for security instead of cost. If, for example, the bottom pins are rounded, then picking them can become more difficult. Rounded pins problematically jam their end slightly beyond the shear line. Unless you stop pushing the pin up with your pick at the exact moment it reaches the shear line, the smaller top portion of the pin will begin to enter the hull. The plug will rotate slightly as the pin continues up past the shear line until the rounded top catches and binds in place. Because the bottom pin is still partially inside the hull, it will keep the plug from rotating. If you apply enough torque, it will remain jammed in place instead of falling down out of the way. If it is the bottom pin that is rounded, you can detect this situation, because the bottom pin will refuse to fall after you have set it. The pins don't have to actually be rounded. As long as the sides of the pin near the shear line are somewhat angled, they can pose a problem and risk jamming while picking.

Beveled holes can pose a similar, though different and challenging, problem. Beveled holes can work together with rounded pins to make picking more difficult for you. As you pick the lock, you will push up on the top pin that is binding in the hope of setting it above the shear line. You listen and feel for the slight clicks that accompany this event. If the plug's holes are beveled, it will cause interesting behavior. As the top pin starts coming close to clearing the shear line, the beveled plug pinholes will give more maneuvering space to the pin. You will feel the plug start to spin slightly. Then, all of a sudden, a different pin might bind now that the plug has turned. You will then have to push the new pin instead of continuing to push on the first pin. This is why beveled holes will sometimes force you to pick the same pin column more than once before you can clear the shear line.

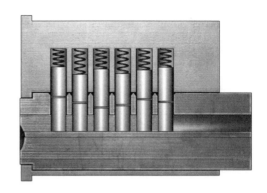

Beveled Plug Holes

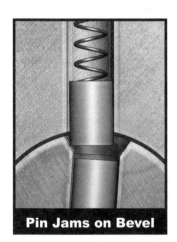

Pin Jams on Bevel

Depending on the configuration of the rounded pins and bevels, you can also get a top pin jammed across the shear line. If this happens, the bottom pin will still fall freely, as if you had set it properly. Lighten up on the torque you are applying and try to push the pins up further for it to set properly. Be careful not to push too hard or too far, as you could subsequently jam the bottom pin instead. If this is the case, you can cause it to fall by easing up on the torque and jiggling the pin slightly to get it to fall down. Rock it back and forth with a pick or rake it lightly. The force of the spring pushing down will help you. You may simply have to pick some of the pin stacks more than once to open the lock. Or, you may have to let go of the torque wrench and start over.

Depending on how rounding and beveling are used, locks can become hard to pick, easier to manufacture, or longer-lasting. You may have to rake or pick certain pins several times for them to set properly. You may have to go back later and pick the pin again, after you have set some other pins and are able to rotate the plug further. Ultimately, your persistence will pay off.

Master Keying

Many installations and buildings might have a large number of different locks. For example, a hotel needs a different lock for each room, of which there can be hundreds or thousands. It would not be practical for the owners or maintenance personnel to carry a different key for each lock. For these situations, there may be a *master key* that can unlock all of the other locks. Or there could be a key that works for all of the maintenance areas for the maintenance staff, and another key that works for all of those locks, in addition to some of the offices, for the security staff, and maybe another key that just works for the public areas and offices for the janitorial stall. There are many possible access schemes. Most of them require more than one key to work for more than one lock. Many apartment buildings, dorms, motels, hospitals, and institutions with a lot of rooms employ these systems.

Picking these locks can actually be easier than a normal pin tumbler design. Locksmiths installing these locks realize this, and, depending on their budget, may also install additional security features. First, let us concentrate on the simple master keyed lock design. These locks have extra pins in their pin stacks between the top pin and the bottom pin. These are often called *master pins, middle pins, spacers, master discs,* or *master wafers.*

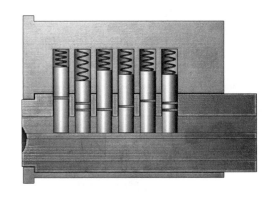

Master Keyed Lock

It is now possible to push the pin stack up to either one of two different heights to put a gap between pins at the shear line and allow the lock to open. This allows for two different keys to open the same lock. A neighboring lock may have the master pin and bottom pin cut differently so the same master key will work, but a different user key is required.

Remember, if you are going to perform maintenance on a master keyed lock, even if you use a plug follower to remove the plug, that some of the middle pins may be in the plug while others may remain in the hull. If you forget about these extra pins in the hull while re-keying, you may cause the lock to function improperly and can reduce its security.

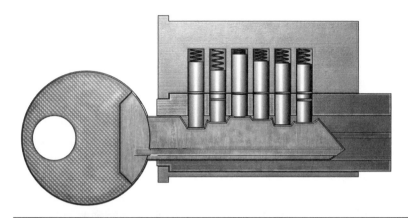

User Key

You also have to be careful about these small middle pins after you have picked the lock. If you spin the plug completely upside down, the small middle pins may fall into the bottom of the keyway and jam. If you turn the plug this far, you must make sure to keep the keyway clear of fallen pins. This is only a concern if your keyway is open on the bottom and the opening is large enough to let all or part of the pin fall through. You can use your pick or other tool in the keyway to keep pins from falling. If they do become a problem, you can always use a broken key extractor or strong magnet to remove them. This means that you will have to replace them for all keys to work again in the lock, so be careful.

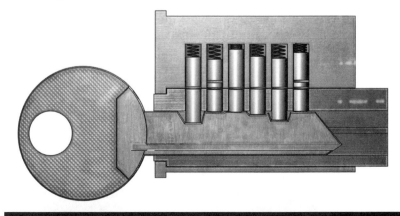

Master Key

Usually, the master key will lift the bottom pin to the shear line while the user key will lift the middle pin to the shear line. This way, the master key will have shallower cuts than any of the user keys. If this were not the case, then a person could simply file down the appropriate cut in a user key to make a more powerful master key.

When dealing with locks that are keyed to work with master keys they can be easier to pick because of the multiple pins. This design allows for more than one key to work the lock, which predictably makes picking it easier. There are more pin height options available, so you are more likely to set the pin at a proper one while picking. If there is only one middle pin, then there are two possible ways to open the lock. With two middle pins, this number already increases to four possibilities. Now, consider more complex master key setups with more middle pins. Three middle pins lead to eight possible combinations. Four middle pins create sixteen possible combinations. Some of these may be unintended combinations for which there is no key. You can, of course, still pick the lock using these possibilities just fine.

The number of possibilities can rise dramatically in more complex installations making them easy pickings. Locksmiths know this as well. That is why some of the pins may be specially shaped in clever ways to trick you. We will cover these special high security pin designs in the next section.

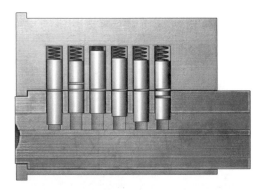

Pickable Option with No Key

Master Key Discovery Technique

If you happen to already have a user key for the lock, then there is an interesting approach to find the master key shape. The master key shape will provide all of the access privileges of the real master key. This approach only requires access to a single lock in the system, that you probably already have access to if you have a user key. The downside of this approach is that it requires a good deal of filing. When performing this discovery technique, you only need to try various keys in the lock as you would try a normal key. No suspicious picks, tools, or actions are required on-site. All of the filing can be performed off-site. However, many key attempts are required, which could mean many trips back to the lock.

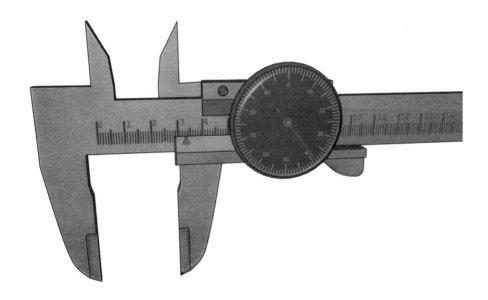

Calipers

Look at the user key that you already have and discern how many pin stacks the lock has. You need to obtain at least as many blank keys that fit your lock as there are pins stacks in the lock. A good file will also be required, and a caliper can help ease some tasks to accurately measure the depths of the various pin grooves on the key.

For now, let us assume there are five pin stacks. In this case you will have five blanks. File them all down so that they almost match the original key.

Original User Key

Notice that each blank has one pin stack position that isn't filed at all, while all other positions are filed to exactly match the original key. You can use calipers to be sure that your cuts precisely match the original key. Leaving one position completely un-filed can sometimes be problematic. If the differences between neighboring pin groove depths is too large, then the key may be impossible to insert all the way into the lock or it may get stuck inside the lock once inserted. The master key will obviously not have cuts that make the key unusable. Therefore, you can safely file some height off the steep sides of pin grooves before running into problems of this nature.

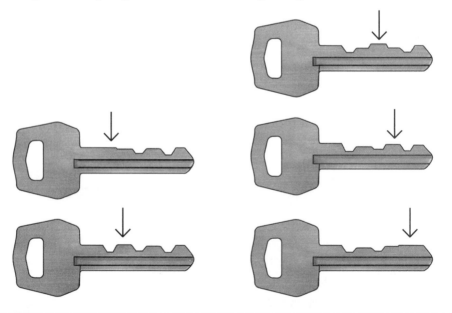

Test Blanks Prepared With Different Test Groove Positions

Now that you have your blanks, it's time to find alternative heights of pin grooves at which the lock will open. Choose a blank, insert it into a lock in the system, and turn it. Most likely, nothing will happen. The position that you left un-filed on this blank is your test position. The goal will be to find out if there are any other depths of this test position that will also work on the lock. Remove the key and file the test pin groove a little and try again. As you file and try different depths, you will eventually reach the pin groove depth of the original key and the lock should open. You can measure with the caliper to make sure that this pin groove depth matches the depth of the corresponding pin groove on the original key. At this point you can move on to another blank and test different depths of other test groove positions. Keep filing down all of your blanks in this fashion; and if the lock opens at a different location than the original key cut, then you found a possible pin depth at which the master lock operates. Measure the depth of the pin groove with the caliper and write it down, along with its location on the key.

Master keys usually have shallower cuts than user keys. This prevents people with user keys from simply filing them down to make master keys. After you have filed your test blanks to the point of the original cut depth you can continue to file the same test pin groove to try depths deeper than the original pin groove. This can be done in case the master key actually has a deeper pin groove at that location.

When you are done filing all of the blanks, there should be at least one key with a different pin groove depth that also works the lock. However, it is also possible that there are more. If there is only one pin groove depth that has an alternative depth, then you already have all the information you need to make the master key. If there are multiple pins with alternate depths, then you might have to file several potential master keys. First, file a key that has all the alternate depths. If the all-alternate depth key doesn't work on other doors under the same master key scheme, then you may need to try making keys with some of the other combinations of original and alternate depths. Some master key systems can be very complex with different master keys working different sets of locks.

High Security Pins

High *security pins* are similar to normal pins – well, almost. They serve the same basic purpose. They are spring-loaded and break at the shear line just like their simpler brethren. Their advantages become apparent when you try to pick them. They will fool you into thinking they have been set, while they haven't cleared the shear line at all. After thinking you have set the pin, you may move on to the next pin, continuing on until you think all of the pins are set. At this point, you will realize that something is amiss when the plug refuses to unlock. It may rotate slightly, but will refuse to open. This is because a security pin has false set too low and is still blocking the shear line.

Example Security Tumblers

Normally, the top pins will have a more or less flat top and flat bottom. They may, of course, be rounded, as discussed in a previous section. Recall that the sides of a normal top pin are smooth. They can easily slide up and down within their designated hole. The sides of security pins will have a modified shape to make picking more difficult. Keep in mind that the illustrations in this section have been greatly exaggerated to emphasize a particular concept.

The *mushroom driver* gets its name because its shape vaguely resembles a mushroom. It can be installed and used just like a normal top pin. The indentation in the side of the pin allows it to false set as it is being pushed up with a pick. The top edge of the head of the pin will make contact with the hull, providing the false set. The top pin will remain bound between the hull and the plug, allowing the bottom pin to fall when pressure from the pick is removed. In reality, the pin column has not yet been raised enough, and the head of the mushroom remains lodged in the plug.

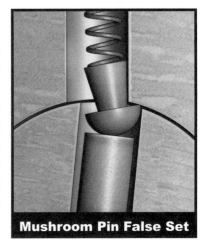

Mushroom Pin False Set

Since the top edge of the head of the mushroom catches on the edge of the hole in the hull, you may be unable to continue pushing the pin up. You can solve this by reducing pressure on your torque wrench. This allows the mushroom pin to fit completely through the hole. The pin may have to be tapped for it to properly and completely set. Fitting the wider head past the shear line and completely into the hull will cause the plug to rotate backward slightly. A sensitive touch or a spring-loaded torque wrench will help to keep an appropriate amount of torque on the rest of the pins. Nevertheless, previously set pins may become loose and unset themselves. Do not worry; you can always go back and easily reset these ordinary pins again.

Mushroom Pin False Set

Some mushroom pins are also rounded. This can provide the additional security accorded to rounded pins. They can cause additional false sets, and you may have to pick them several times for them to properly set.

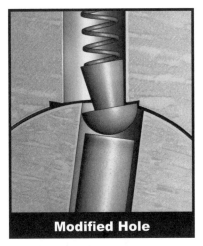

Modified Hole

Manufacturers can also widen the upper portion of the pin hole in the hull. This allows the top pin to angle more and increases the chances that it will catch. An edge or chamfer can also be made at the opening to the hole in the hull. This makes it easier for the head of the modified top pin to catch on this lip.

A second popular design for high security pins is the *spool pin*. They are designed to provide a very deceiving false set. Similar to the mushroom pin, the bottom of the pin is wider than the middle. It can also be very difficult to detect their presence until it is too late. The side of the pin is designed to catch at the shear line. The end of the spool can catch on the hole entering the hull, making it very difficult to push up while applying torque to the plug. You can deal with spool pins the same as mushroom pins. Release some torque tension to

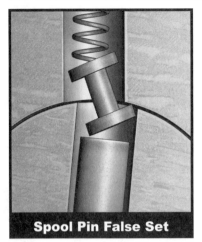

Spool Pin False Set

allow you to slip the wider portion of the pin past the shear line. Again, releasing pressure may cause other pin stacks to unset. The important part is that you have set the security pin; since the other pin that fell was binding first, it should be easier to reset. It can be more difficult when setting a security pin causes another previously set pin to unset, and resetting the latter causes the former to unset. Make sure that you only release just as much torque as you need, and no more.

Sometimes, the top or bottom pin may actually have a smaller radius. This can create some odd effects while picking. For example, if the bottom pin is larger than the top one, it can bind with the hull, even though the top pin might be too small to catch on the plug and set until you are able to rotate the plug further. If the bottom pin is smaller, it may behave differently after you set the pin column. The bottom pin could be small enough to fit past the shear line, even though the top pin has set. In this situation, you can often push the bottom pin past the shear line and up into the hull. Instead of hitting the hull and stopping, you can feel the spring's resistance. Nevertheless, when you lower your pick, the top pin will again rest on the plug at the shear line.

An important difference between opening a lock with its key and picking it open is that a torque must be applied to the plug while picking. There is a pin design that exploits this fact to make picking incredibly difficult. The *serrated pin* has many grooves cut into its sides. The sides of the holes in the plug and hull have one or more corresponding teeth or edges that fit into the grooves of the pin. This effectively locks the pin in place, preventing you from sliding it up or down.

Some prefer to *reverse pick* locks with modified pins. This is accomplished by using a heavy torque and pushing all of the top pins up past the shear line. After doing this, all of the top pins will be completely inside the hull and the bottom pins will be binding at the shear line. Use your rake or pick and rake across the pins to vibrate each of the pins, while simultaneously reducing torque. Hopefully, every pin will lower to its shear line. Because the modified top pins remain safely in the hull the entire time, they do not upset this method. A diamond pick is recommended for this method. As long as all of the modified pins remain in the hull, it should be relatively easy to later pick the normal pins if they lower too much.

Generally, only a few of the top pins will be replaced with special, high-security pins. The first pin column will almost never use a security pin. An exception to this is the serrated pin design, which can be used in all pin columns. If pushing on the pins causes the plug to rotate slightly backwards, then you are likely dealing with a modified high-security pin. Employ a light torque applied to the torque wrench and a heavier force pushing on the pins with your pick. As most of these designs rely on you applying a torque to the plug while picking, you may find vibration or impact picking more effective. Security tumblers were once exclusively the domain of expensive high-security cylinders. As time goes on, they are becoming more and more common. It is now quite likely that you will experience them in your travels.

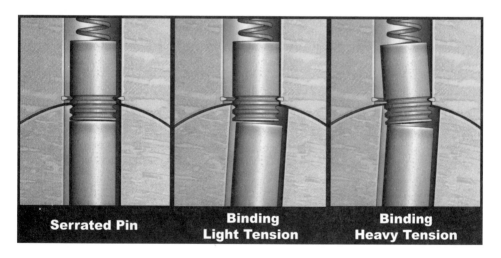

Serrated Pin   **Binding Light Tension**   **Binding Heavy Tension**

Tension Tools

There are actually a wide variety of tension tools available. We discussed the basic torque wrench, but there are others that can make lock picking a little bit easier, fit better with a unique lock style, or might just fit better with your picking style. A simple example of these specialty tools are the *round tension tools*. These tools often have two **L** shaped metal wires. The tips of these wires go into the top and bottom of the keyway.

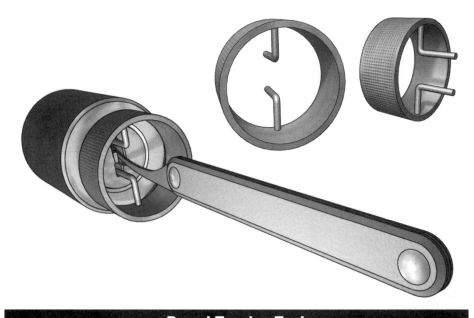

Round Tension Tool

With these tension tools it is possible to rotate the plug in either direction with equal ease. Unlike the traditional torque wrench, this tool is also less likely to interfere with or be disturbed by the action of a pick or rake. The torque that this tool provides can be more balanced than the regular torque wrench, because the two points where pressure is applied are on the opposing far ends of the keyhole. The simplest of these round tension tools has a fixed distance between the two L-shaped wires. More advanced models allow the user to match the exact shape of the keyway by altering the distance between the wires. These improved versions have a spring-loaded button that is pressed to bring the two wires closer. The tool is then inserted into the keyway and the button is let go. The spring pushes the wires apart until both wires are pressing on the opposite sides of the keyway.

Spring-loaded round tension tools are also available. These tools allow you to exactly control the amount of torque that you apply to the plug. Many of these tools come with a dial that shows exactly how much tension the spring is providing. The spring inside of the tool absorbs some of the tension that you provide, so the total output of torque is less than what you put in. This property allows the user to have more exact control over how much tension is applied. Fine control of tension is especially necessary when picking advanced pin tumblers with modified pins. With those locks, it is quite likely that a pin could false set, only to be discovered when pushing on the pin causes the plug to counter-rotate. In such cases, tensions should be slowly decreased while pushing up on the pin that false set. If torque is eased too rapidly, then some of the other previously set pins will fall back down into the plug. This design could make it harder to notice when a pin column has set, however, because the spring dampens the slight and sudden plug rotation that happens when the top pin crosses the shear line. It is still possible to observe this event on the torque dial. Preference to use this style of torque wrench really depends on your style, how developed your sense of touch is, how visual you are, etc…

Spring-loaded Round Tension Tool

There are other spring-loaded torque wrench designs that are not round, and more classical in form. This particular spring tension wrench is useful when picking advanced pin tumblers for the same reasons as the round spring tension wrench. Unlike its round cousin, this tool doesn't have a visual indicator to help you notice when the column has set; therefore, this tool demands a bit more skill.

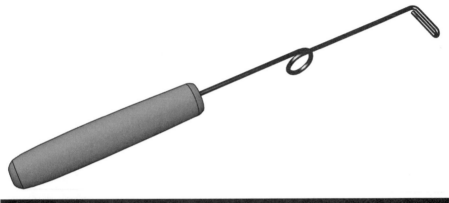

Spring-loaded Torque Wrench

There are other classical tension wrenches that can adjust to various keyholes and grip them from opposite sides. These tension wrenches are especially useful for double-sided wafer locks, but they can often be used with standard pin tumbler locks as well. Just like the round tension tools, they attempt to minimally interfere with the pick, regardless of the keyhole size.

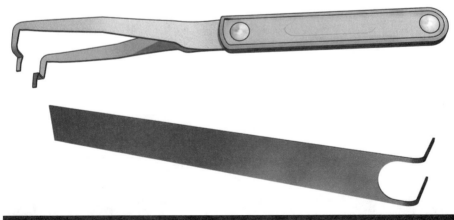

Double-sided Torque Wrenches

Plug Spinner

As you work with various locks, you will find that each lock has its own personality. Remember the misalignment in the pins that causes them to bind in a certain order? Well that means that if you pick a lock clockwise, the pins will bind in the opposite order than if you picked it counter-clockwise. Sometimes one direction of rotation will be much easier to pick than the other. This is not always a problem if the easier direction is the way you want to turn it in the first place, or if the lock can be turned in either direction. At other times, it may be a problem if the easier direction to pick is the wrong direction. Many locks will only let you unlock them in one direction. You may find yourself in a situation where you worked hard to pick a lock only to find that you are turning the plug the wrong way. In such cases, you can use a tool called a *plug spinner* to quickly rotate the plug past the locking position and to the open position. An example of one common style of plug spinner is depicted below. Since the plug spinner spins the plug at very high speeds past the locking point, the spring-loaded top pins don't have enough time to fall into their holes within the plug. This keeps the plug from locking and allows you to pick the lock in the easier, albeit "wrong," direction.

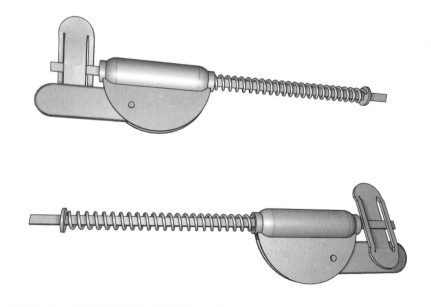

Plug Spinner

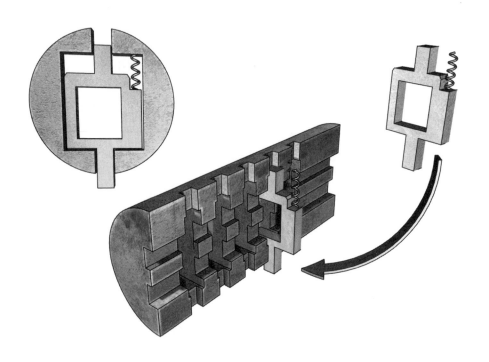

4

Wafer Locks

Wafer Tumbler Locks

The *wafer tumbler lock*, or *disc tumbler*, is quite common in low-cost applications because of their lower manufacturing cost. Introduced at the end of the 1800's, they can be found on desks, filing cabinets, car doors, windows, older vending machines, and fire security boxes, among other things. They are very similar to pin tumblers, except they use wafers instead of round pins. In fact, if you wish, you may mostly ignore this chapter and use the techniques you have previously learned. It is generally agreed that a comparable wafer lock is easier to pick than its pin tumbler equivalent.

From the exterior, wafer locks appear similar to pin tumblers, and their keys can look almost identical. The most distinctive feature used to distinguish between them are the wafers. If you look inside the keyway, you will notice wide, flat wafers instead of round pins. The internal workings of a wafer lock, however, are quite different.

Wafer locks work by raising and lowering wafers inside the plug. As the wafers are moved up, they will protrude out of the top of the plug and into a notch in the hull, locking it in place. As they are moved down, they will protrude out of the bottom of the plug and will also lock it in place. The wafers are cut differently, so that each of them has to be moved to a different height for them not to protrude out of the plug. As soon as no wafers are protruding out of the rotating cylinder, it will be free to rotate and unlock.

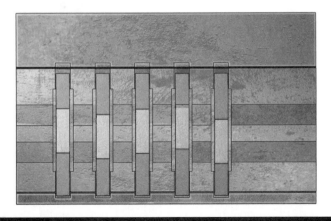

Side view of Wafer Lock

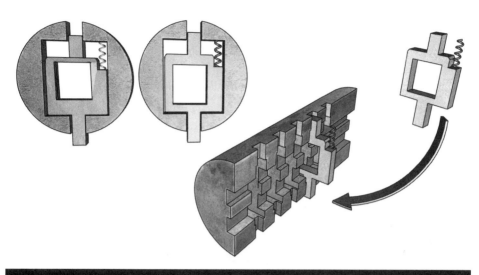

Cutaway view of Wafers in Plug

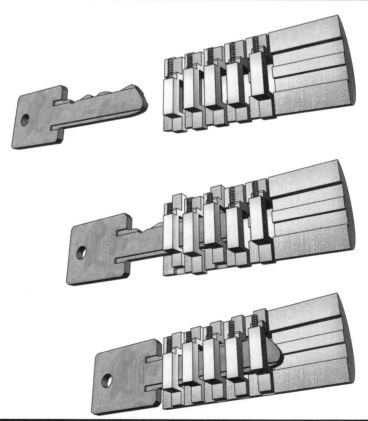

Cutaway view of Plug with Key

Double-Sided Wafer Locks

In an attempt to increase their security, manufacturers devised the *double-sided wafer lock*, or *double-bitted disc tumbler*. Many automobile locks use double-sided wafers. They can also be found on doorknobs, vending machines, office furniture, and anywhere greater security than just a simple wafer lock is needed. They are easy to distinguish by their keys, which have ridges on both sides. The wafers have alternating springs. Some will have to be pushed up while others will need to be pushed down. Some locks have the same sequence of tumblers on each side which allows the key to be inserted either way; this is called a *convenience key*. Other locks have a different pattern on each side for slightly higher security.

Here is where your set of double-sided picks will come in handy. You can push up on some wafers, and then easily push down, without having to turn the pick upside-down. The double-sided picks shown here will also work well for some brands of doubled-sided locks. The special dual-pronged torque wrench pictured here is common in many kits and is specifically designed for double-sided locks. This is used in conjunction with the double-sided picks shown in Chapter 2. It allows you to rotate the plug and will let you insert the pick into the middle of the keyway. This gives you easier access to both the top and bottom wafers.

If you have already learned pin tumblers and wafer locks, then you will find double-sided locks are a straightforward extension of what you already know.

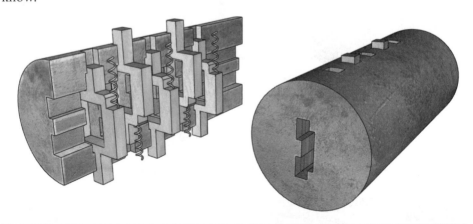

Cutaway view of Plug with Alternating Wafers

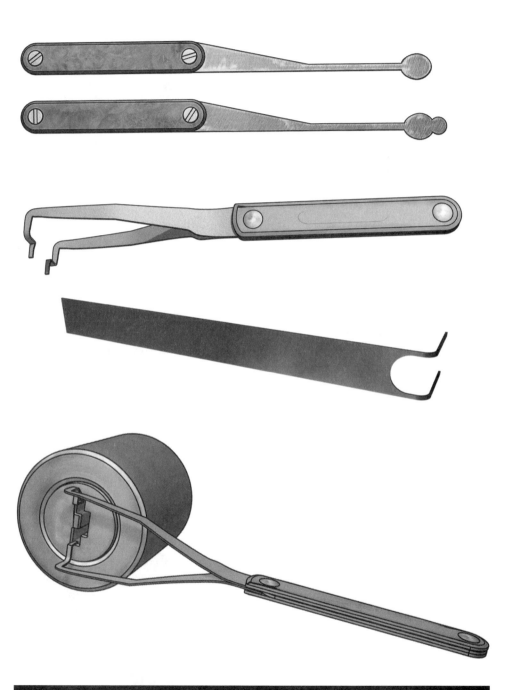

Picks and Torque Wrenches for Double-Sided Locks

Plate wafer locks increase security by using a high number of wafers. They often employ more than ten wafers in a single lock.

Side bar wafer locks further increase security by utilizing a bar that will only fall into place once all of the wafers are aligned. This makes it difficult to set each wafer individually. Picking this type of lock usually requires that some force be applied to the side bar to push it into the tumblers. This allows you to bind the wafers and keep them in place once they are picked into position.

Picking Wafer Locks

When picking wafer locks, the same techniques that you used for pin tumblers may be used. Due to their nature, some tools were developed specifically for wafer locks. One such tool is the *jiggler* or *tryout key.* A locksmith might have a large collection of such keys, which are essentially pieces of metal that vaguely resemble actual keys. They vary widely in shape so that if one does not work, then the next one might. You can obtain a set of tryout keys that target a specific type of lock. If lock tolerances are poor, the key can be cut at a depth halfway between two official heights and work for either one in the lock. This drastically reduces the possible key combinations. In fact, before 1968, an appropriate set of only 64 tryout keys could open any GM automotive lock. The concept is simple—insert the jiggler key and try it out. Jiggle it around and move it up and down while attempting to turn it with a slight bit of force. If it doesn't work, go on to the next. If that does not work, then try the next. Try several tryout keys. Your probability of success varies and depends on the type and quality of lock, the shapes of your keys, how many keys you have, how they are jiggled, your experience, and luck.

With some experience you will find that wafer locks are generally easier to pick than pin tumblers. Remember that the wafers can be much thinner and closer to each other than pins. This may make it harder to lift individual wafers without disturbing its neighbors; using a pick that can more easily slide from wafer to wafer, however, can make raking much easier.

Double-Sided Jigglers

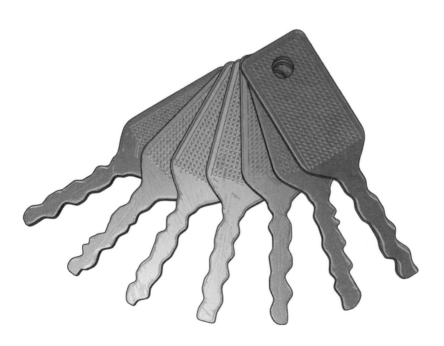

Tryout Keys

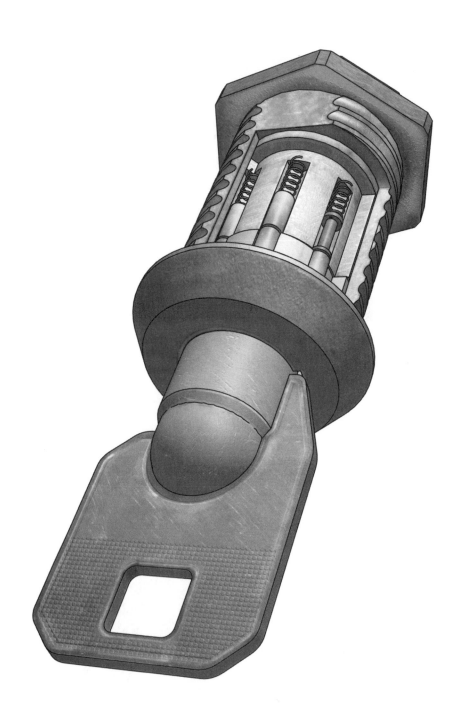

5

Tubular Locks

Tubular Locks

The invention of the *tubular lock* brought a vast improvement over traditional pin tumbler designs. In the early 1930's, as the Great Depression set in, pin tumbler locks were common and were often used on publicly available coin-operated machines. As the Depression brought desperation, lock picking techniques became widespread among thieves. Around this time, a small Chicago company developed and was granted a patent for the tubular lock in 1934. They initially marketed their locks to high-security fields that were in dire need of a superior lock. They have since become commonplace on vending machines and portable locks in theft-prone areas because of their resistance to amateur picking.

Tubular locks essentially use the same basic principles as pin tumbler locks, except that their pin and key arrangements are different. Since pin tumblers and tubular locks are so similar, you could theoretically utilize similar techniques to pick each kind. In reality, though, their keyhole and pin layouts make using the same tools very difficult. Also, because of their design, the tubular locks would relock every $1/8^{th}$ of a turn. Once you had managed to pick all of the pins successfully and began rotating the inner cylinder, it would turn slightly and then, frustratingly, relock in a new position. You would have to pick all of the pins again and repeat the entire process seven or eight times. A word of caution before you try this: many locks will not allow you to insert the actual key when the shaft is rotated in an intermediate position. This means you will have to pick it completely to the fully locked or fully unlocked position before you can operate the lock normally again. The tubular lock was considered a very high-security lock; that is, until the day the tubular lock pick became available. With the arrival of tubular lock picks, the task of compromising a tubular lock suddenly became a much quicker and easier undertaking. Since the introduction of effective picking tools, the race between lock manufacturers and the lock picking industry has never ended. With some skill, the right tools, and a lot of practice, you should be able to open many of the tubular locks in use.

Please review the earlier chapeters on pin tumblers before diving into this chapter. Tubular locks build on the concepts discussed with traditional pin tumblers.

How Tubular Locks Work

As always, before jumping in and learning the picking techniques, it helps to become familiar with how the lock you are trying to pick actually works. First, let's get familiar with the names and locations of the various pieces that make up this style of lock.

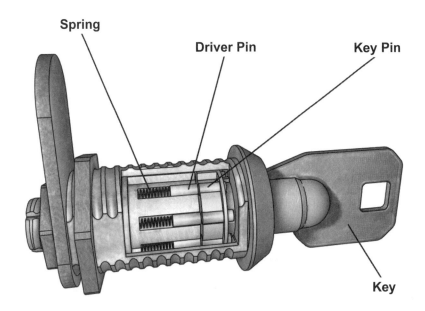

Parts of a Tubular Lock

In this sideways cutaway view, you will notice that there are two pins and a spring that make up each pin stack. This is exactly like the pin tumbler lock described in Chapter 2. Tubular locks work in a very similar fashion to the traditional pin tumbler. Confusingly, the conventional name for the pins that touch the key in tubular locks are called top pins, even though in standard pin tumbler locks, the top pins touch the spring instead of the key. Let's call the tubular top pins *key pins* for simplicity. The pins that touch the spring will be called *driver pins*. It should help to remember the tubular lock pin names for the following explanations.

The theory behind the tubular lock is essentially the same as the pin tumbler. The separation between the key and driver pins must be moved to the shear line to allow them to separate and rotate the plug. The main difference is that instead of the pin stacks being lined up in a row progressively deeper into the lock, they are arranged in a circle with all key pins facing out. This means

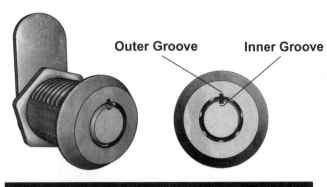

Tubular Lock Keyway

that, instead of a long key with notches of varying depths, it uses a round key with notches of varying depths. The notches are evenly placed around the circumference of the key. When the key is inserted, all pin stacks are manipulated simultaneously. Just like the pin tumbler, the notch depths have to match the lengths of the key pins, so the break between the driver pin and the key pin line up with the shear line. When all the pin stacks are lined up with the shear line, the inner cylinder is free to rotate – just like the pin tumbler! If you have not already done so, we recommend reviewing the

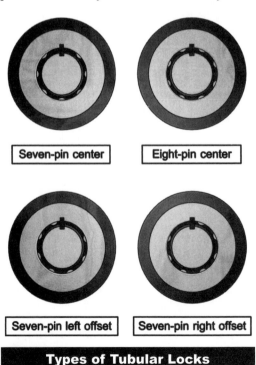

Types of Tubular Locks

chapter on pin tumblers, which explains this concept in greater detail.

Now let's take a closer look at that keyway. If you look straight into the keyway, you will see a round opening usually with seven or eight pins neatly distributed inside. You won't be able to see the face of the pins in their entirety. That's because the front of the lock holds them in place and keeps them from being pushed out by the springs. While there are now plenty of styles, the vast majority of tubular locks come in one of these four varieties.

As you will learn later, the distribution of the pins will determine the appropriate lock picking tool you should use.

Some other features of the lock design that you should take note of are the protrusions on the key, and the extra grooves in the lock. The inner key protrusion goes inside the inner lock groove. And, as you've probably guessed, the outer key protrusion goes inside the outer lock groove. Each protrusion has its own purpose. The inner protrusion causes the key to rotate the inner cylinder when it is turned. This, in turn, unlocks the lock. The outer protrusion, on the other hand, helps to ensure that the user correctly uses the key. It prevents the key from being removed unless the lock is turned completely to the locked or unlocked position. It is not absolutely necessary to work the lock, but it helps make sure it is never left in an intermediate position. The available picking tools have an equivalent of an inner protrusion, but lack the outer protrusion completely. The outer protrusion forces the user to insert the key in a certain orientation, and then prevents the user from removing the key until one full rotation is completed, or until another outer groove is reached. Many locks have only one outer groove and require a complete turn to lock or unlock. Others have two outer grooves, and you only need to turn the key from one outer groove to another. Another kind of lock has only one outer groove, yet only needs to be partially rotated to unlock. The key cannot be removed from these locks when they are unlocked. If you happen to file off the outer protrusion on your key, you would be able to insert the key, turn it halfway, and then remove it. A half–turned inner cylinder is only halfway picked. The key pins align themselves exactly over the driver pins every $1/8^{th}$ or $1/7^{th}$ of a turn, depending on how many pin stacks there are. As soon as that happens, the driver pins jump above the shear line, thus blocking further rotation and relocking the inner cylinder in place.

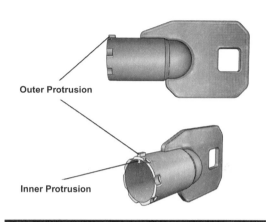

Tubular Lock Key

Picking Tubular Locks

The first specialty tools locksmiths used to pick tubular locks worked on principles similar to raking. Lock manufacturers caught on, though, and countermeasures were soon implemented. Today, successfully defeating many tubular locks usually means applying tools that work on the principle of picking individual pin stacks. We will first cover the raking method, and then we will introduce more advanced tools, techniques, and countermeasures that have been developed. Remember, tubular locks were designed to provide increased security over the common pin tumbler. Therefore, expect them to be much harder to pick than your common deadbolt. It will take time and lots of practice to get just the right touch. Read through and understand all the concepts before diving in.

Picking tubular locks is also harder than traditional locks because the tools are highly specialized, more expensive, and harder to improvise. Tools come in a wide variety of styles. They range from just mildly expensive to complex devices that resemble surgical equipment and cost just as much. You need to use one that matches the size and pin arrangement of your target lock. No matter how advanced the tubular lock design happens to be, you will have to start by identifying the geometry of the lock before you apply any lock picking tool. Tubular lock picking tools usually have levers that can slide in and out. These levers are called *feelers*. The most common tubular picks have eight or seven equally distributed feelers.

Feeler

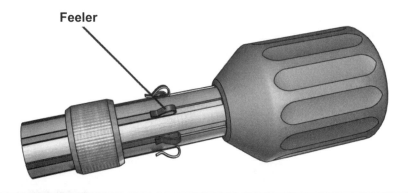

Tubular Lock Pick

It's easy to determine which tool to use: simply look at the face of the lock. Seven-pin left offset, seven-pin right offset, and eight-pin center share the same pin geometry, and you should use an eight-feeler pick on them. You may ask yourself why you would want to use an eight-feeler pick on a seven-pin lock. The feelers must align themselves exactly over the pins. In the case of seven-pin left and right offset, the seven pins are arranged as if eight pins were equally distributed around the lock except that the pin to the right or left of the outer groove is missing. The position of the feeler that corresponds to the empty space is irrelevant to the picking of the lock.

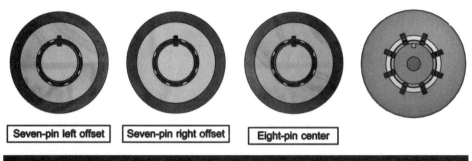

| Seven-pin left offset | Seven-pin right offset | Eight-pin center |

Lock Types that use the Eight-feeler Pick

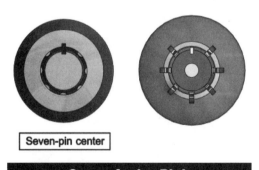

Seven-pin center

Seven-feeler Pick

Only the more common seven-pin center style will make use of the seven-feeler pick.

When you successfully pick a tubular lock using a tubular lock pick, many tools allow you to lock the feelers in place. When you are done, the feelers are moved into positions that reflect the notch depth cuts in the actual key. The picking tool can then be used like a regular key. It is even possible to use additional tools to read the position of the locked feelers on the pick and cut a new tubular key to match the lock.

Raking Method

The raking technique has an advantage since each individual feeler does not need to be manipulated. You should know that many modern locks implement countermeasures that prevent the racking technique from really working. Don't be surprised, then, if many locks do not open when you try this method.

The first step is to line up the feelers against the tip of the picking tool. Just push the feelers out past the end of the pick, then hold the tool and push it against a flat surface so that all of the feelers retreat flush with the tip of the tool.

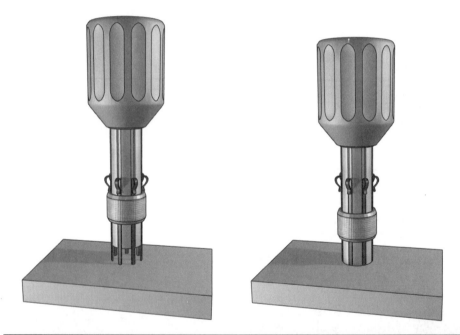

Push feelers against flat surface

Once the feelers are correctly positioned, push the pick completely into the lock. Make sure that the picking tool remains completely lined up with the lock while you do this. Don't tilt the picking tool; keep it lined up with the lock throughout the entire procedure.

If you tilt the pick, you will probably be unsuccessful. Imagine that you are very close to having almost all of the feelers set to the appropriate key depths. Almost all of the key pins would be resting on the shear line and almost all of the feelers would be set to the appropriate height. If you tilted the pick to one side, some of the feelers would be pushed further up by the key pins that are set and resting on the shear line. When you straighten out the pick again, the correctly-set feelers would no longer accurately reflect the proper key cut. If you have already set all of the pins and tilt the pick while rotating it, then when you turn the pick $1/7^{th}$ or $1/8^{th}$ of the way, the key pins will be pushed out by the springs. When that happens, you will have to deal with a lock that is stuck in an intermediate position. The proper key cannot be inserted because of the outer notch. You will have to start over and pick it again, but this time be careful not to tilt the tool.

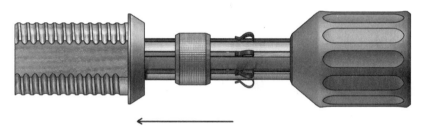

Insert pick straight into lock

Once you insert the pick inside the lock, you will have to effectively control the pick with careful and delicate movements. Correctly handling the pick is crucial to being able to pick successfully. It is a tricky skill to learn, but don't lose hope. Don't just grab the pick and wield it as if you were going to stab someone. Instead, hold the handle as if you were about to write with a very large pen. Now that you have inserted the pick into the lock, you will have to slightly push the pick in and out of the lock about one-eighth to one-sixteenth of an inch. While you are pushing the pick in and out, remember to keep the pick lined up with the lock. The trick is that you must always apply a slight turning tension to the pick, as if you were trying to turn the key. We'll cover this in more detail after explaining spring strength. The turning pressure creates torque on the inner cylinder, just like the torque wrench did when working a normal pin tumbler. After repeated pushing and pulling of your pick, the lock should open. Many locks will have countermeasures to prevent your job from being this simple. Cheaper or older locks, however, can open quite quickly.

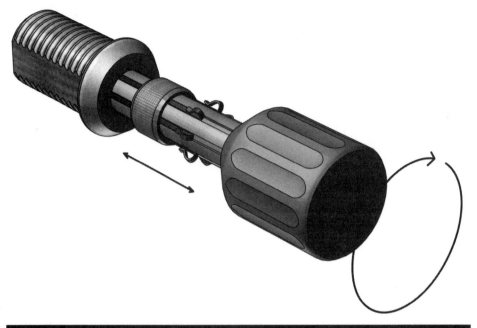

Slide in and out slightly while applying torque

Different locks have different types of springs in them. In fact, modern locks may have several different spring types in just one lock. If the feelers slide in and out of the pick easily and the springs in the lock are very strong, then you won't be able to use the pick as-is. You will have to adjust the feelers so that they are harder to slide in and out. Many tools are adjustable, and can be tightened with a twist, Allen wrench, or some other means. Sometimes you will have to jury-rig the tool by tightening a rubber band or two around the feelers.

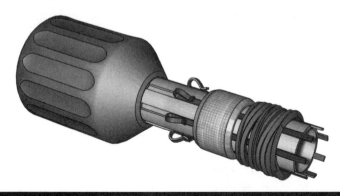

Increase tension on the feelers if needed

On the other hand, if the feelers are too difficult to slide, then the feelers will simply push the key pins past the shear line and prevent you from raking. The feelers need to be strong enough to push against the spring, but weak enough to allow the pin to set and move the feeler. The ease with which the feelers slide in and out should be proportional to the spring strength. You can test the spring strength with one of picks. Simply press the tip of your pick against the exposed portion of the key pin inside the tubular lock. As you push the key pin, you are effectively pushing against the pin and can feel the strength of the spring in the back of that pin column. The stronger the spring, the harder you should make it for the feelers to move. Test the strength of each spring. If all the springs have about the same strength, then the lock can be picked with this raking technique. However, if the springs are of noticeably different strengths, then different tools and techniques may be needed.

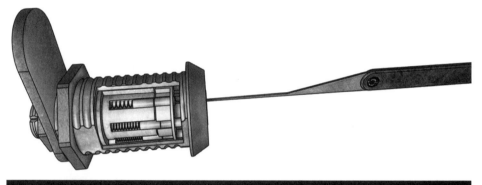

Test the various springs' strengths

Let's take a look at why spring strength matters so much. As you push the pick inside the lock, just like a blank key, the feelers should push the key pins inward. When this happens, all of the driver pins will be pushed below the shear line. If the feelers can slide in and out too easily, and the spring strength is high enough, then this will not work. Instead, the springs will push back on the driver and key pins, and cause the feelers to slide out all the way until the pick resembles a key with deepest cuts. If the feelers slide too stiffly, then they will not allow the pins to set. Further jiggling in and out would contribute nothing and waste your time. Tightening or loosing the resistance of the feelers will be needed. When the feelers are correctly set, you'll be back in business. If the springs are of different strengths, move on to the next section describing individual pin manipulation.

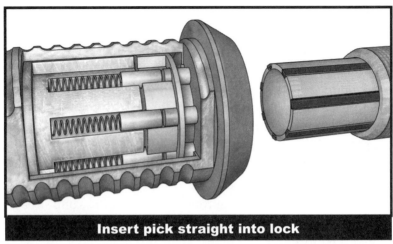

Insert pick straight into lock

Once we have established that the spring strengths are appropriate, we can start to actually rake the lock. When you first insert the pick, don't apply any torque. Simply slide it all the way in, straight and without any rotation. Once all the way in, you can apply the slight rotational torque and slide the tool in and out. You don't have to move it completely out each time; that would just make things more difficult. Rather, only slide it out as much as the deepest possible key pin length or key notch depth. Continue applying the turning tension the entire time and be careful not to turn too hard or soft. The turning tension you apply will cause one of the pin columns to bind,

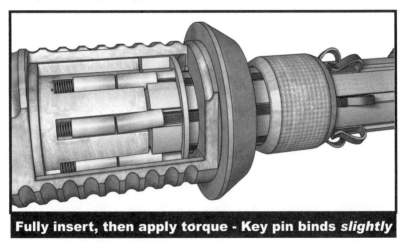

Fully insert, then apply torque - Key pin binds *slightly*

just like the pin tumbler. If your turning tension is just right, then you can still push the binding pin into the lock with the feeler and the spring can still push it out. You may wonder what the point of this weak turning tension is if the pins are still able to move. As you slide the tool outward, the binding key pin completely crosses the shear line and is entirely on one side; then the turning tension will cause the inner lock cylinder to turn slightly. At this point, the driver pin will be kept in place by the lock cylinder. The edge of the hole that moved slightly when the cylinder turned will hold the pin back.

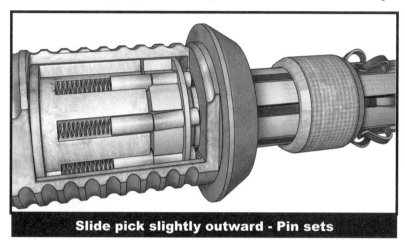

Slide pick slightly outward - Pin sets

This pin column is now set. Since the key pin can't go back further into the lock, the key pin will resist and push back on the feeler. When you start to push the pick back in, the key pin causes the feeler for this pin column to start sliding back as the tool continues to slide in the rest of the way.

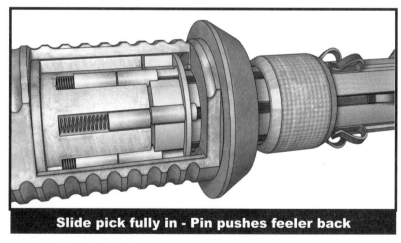

Slide pick fully in - Pin pushes feeler back

Before the column was set, the feeler was pushing against the pins and the spring. The feeler resistance was strong enough to move the spring, but now the feeler is pushing against the key pin which is set and resting against the shear line. The feeler resistance should not be able to resist this solid connection and will be pushed back. When the pick is pushed completely into the lock, the feeler will be pushed back exactly the length of the key pin! If the feelers are too hard to move, you might forcefully slide the key pin back across the shear line and rotate the lock slightly backwards. That is why it is so important to get the feeler resistance just right. Simply repeat this process until all of the pins are set, and the lock will rotate. As each pin stack sets, the next pin stack will bind.

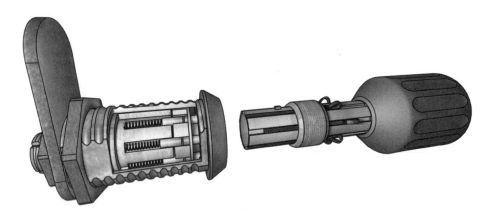

Example with one feeler set. Set all feelers before removing

As you can see, the feelers can't be too easy to move, since the springs could then push them up. They also can't be too hard to move, since then they could overcome the turning tension and push the set key pins back past the shear line. The feelers must, therefore, be set proportional to the strength of the springs. Your pick probably has some mechanism devised to give the feelers some resistance. The example tool here has a brass ring wrapping around the feelers.

Underneath this brass ring is a stretched rubber O-ring that keeps the feelers from easily sliding in and out. The O-rings are specifically selected to press down on the feelers just enough to work with a majority of the locks. If you wrap additional rubber bands around the feelers, you will clamp them down further. Rubber bands may apply equally to all feelers, or they may slide around and provide inconsistent friction. A more sophisticated tool may be required if this is a problem.

To prevent this raking technique, many locks will have different spring strengths in each pin stack. Since you can't individually apply pressure to each feeler, it's very difficult to use this raking technique with a tubular lock that has variable spring strengths. Even if you have a tool with variable feeler resistance for each feeler, you would still have to vary the turning tension proportional to the spring strength of the currently binding pin stack. Remember, you need to apply enough turning pressure so the key pin will catch on the edge of the hole and set properly, but not so much that the spring will not push the pin back up as the tool moves out of the lock. Varying the turning tension according to the spring strength of the currently binding pin stack is very difficult, since you have to know which stack is binding and the strength of that particular spring. For these reasons, you will likely have to employ the individual pin manipulation technique described in the next section.

Individual Pin Manipulation Method

Individual pin manipulation is a newer, more effective lock picking method that works against most modern tubular locks. This method requires its own tools, as well as techniques. Make sure the picks that you obtain clearly state that they are suitable for individual pin manipulation. If you are worried about purchasing yet another tool, then rest assured that almost all tubular individual pin manipulation tools can also perform the tubular raking technique that was presented earlier.

Raise all feelers

The individual pin manipulation picks look very similar, though slightly different, from the cheaper and less effective tools that might be sufficient for raking. The example pick pictured above actually needs an Allen wrench to work properly. The Allen wrench is used to control the feeler tension as well as manipulate the feelers that slide in and out. The principles of picking tubular locks by manipulating individual pins are very similar to picking pin tumbler locks.

When getting started, unlike the case of tubular lock raking, you should raise all of the feelers so that when you insert the pick, none of them touch the key pins.

Now insert the pick and apply some turning tension in the direction that the key would turn when opening the lock. Most tubular lock keys rotate clockwise when unlocking. As the correct amount

Insert pick straight into lock

of tension is applied, one of the pin stacks will bind. All of the driver pins will be raised above the shear line, crossing the boundary. Note that with the raking method, it was the key pins that were

Apply torque to bind a driver pin

binding. With the individual pin manipulation method, it is the driver pins that do the binding. One of these driver pins will be first to bind; it is your job to discover which one. To do this, simply lower the feelers into their pin stacks, one by one. Start with the feeler closest to the inner protrusion and then just keep going clockwise. Push each feeler down until the driver pin is forced back below the shear line. If this is indeed the pin stack that

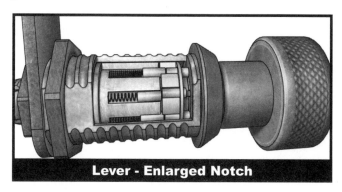

Lever - Enlarged Notch

is binding, then when the driver pin crosses the shear line, the pin stack will set. You will feel the pick turn ever so slightly, and you may hear or feel a slight click. If you don't feel or hear anything, this stack may not be binding. If it moves freely, as if only the spring is resisting you, then another stack is binding or you are not applying enough turning tension.

On the other hand, if this pin stack and others are difficult to depress, then you may be applying too much tension. As soon as you suspect that you have set a pin stack, remove the pick from the lock. Look at the feeler. If the feeler is at, or just barely below, the tip of the pick, then you probably didn't set that pin stack. Once you find the pin stack that set first, write it down.

Raise all feelers

The lock has begun to reveal its secrets; you know which stack sets first. Reset the tool by lifting all of the feelers up again, except for the one corresponding to the first pin stack. Your job is now to find the second pin stack that binds and record it. After you set the second pin stack, reset all feelers except for the first and now second setting stacks. Just repeat this procedure until you know the order in which all the pin stacks set. When you know this, you will know which sequence to press the feelers in order to open the lock.

It is now finally time to pick the lock. Insert the reset tool completely. Depress each feeler in the correct order, setting each pin stack. When you set the last one, the inner cylinder will begin to rotate. Try to stop turning before completing $1/7^{th}$ or $1/8^{th}$ of a turn. If you continue to turn, each of the key pins would align above the next driver pin in the neighboring stack and could, inadvertently, be pushed out by the driver pins and springs. Now is a good time to tighten the feelers of your tool if possible..

Keyway picked, partially rotated

After You Have Picked the Lock

After you have picked the lock by either the raking or the individual pin-manipulation method, remove the tool. Once you pull out the pick, you can measure the heights to which the feelers are set. Most tubular lock pick tools come with a simple *decoder tool* to do this. It often looks like a straight key with large flat notches of increasing depth. Each notch is numbered. Line up the depressed feelers to the tool and see which notch depth matches. That number represents the depth of the notch for that position in the key. Make sure not to disturb the feelers while measuring them. When you have measured the height to which each feeler was pushed in, you will be able to actually produce a key for that lock. While it is nice to make a real key for the lock, this requires a tubular key cutting machine and is not required to simply open the lock. You simply need to immobilize the feelers on the pick and use the pick itself as a key. Some picks come with a small screw on their top that can be turned to hold all of the feelers in place.

Tubular decoder tool

High Security Tubular Locks

The eternal struggle between lock manufacturers and lock picking locksmiths continues. For a while, tubular locks were considered extremely secure. These tools and picking techniques soon developed. Lock manufacturers, of course, were aware of this and have started to incorporate higher security pin tumbler features into their tubular locks. Just as advanced pin tumblers can be defeated with sophisticated techniques, so, too, can these high-security tubular locks.

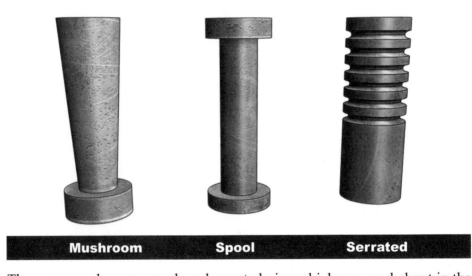

| Mushroom | Spool | Serrated |

The same mushroom, spool, and serrated pins which you read about in the advanced pin tumbler chapter make an appearance in advanced tubular locks. Mushroom and spool pins usually replace the driver pins. It is interesting to note that if all the driver pins were replaced with advanced pins, it would affect picking more than the raking technique. This is because the raking method attempts to keep the driver pins below the shear line. Individual pin picking moves each driver pin past the shear line while applying torque. This means there are lots of opportunities to false set. The raking method doesn't apply torque when first inserting the tool, so the advanced pins don't false set. Once you start applying torque and moving the tool out, it is the key pins that are crossing the shear line, not the driver pins. Since it is usually the driver pins that have the extra security features, you should have fewer problems. Of course, if the key pin of the currently binding pin stack is long, you will need to pull out the tool by at least as much. The next pin stack to bind might have a shorter key pin. If that's the case, then this new

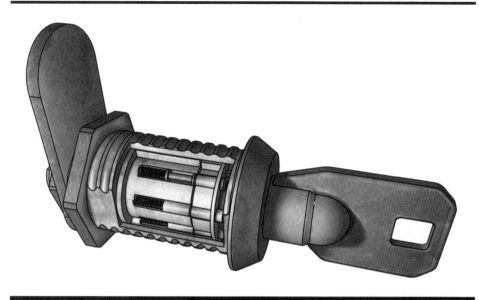

Tubular lock with spool driver pin

driver pin could still false set while it is being pushed back in. But as long as the advanced pins don't cross the shear line, they can't false set. Those who install modified pins are obviously concerned about security, and for this reason, will almost always install variable springs along with advanced pins.

Since only a few positions will probably have mushroom or spool pins, your first task will be to identify locations where these traps lay. Simply pick the lock until you press on a feeler and notice that the pick wants to rotate in the opposite direction of your turning tension. Once you encounter this situation, you may be dealing with a spool or mushroom pin. At this point, release some tension and try to push that pin further, just as you did when you picked the pin tumbler locks with spool or mushroom pins. The tubular pick has a distinct advantage over the classic pin tumbler when it comes to these pin types. You do not have to worry about other pins sliding back across the shear line when you release some tension and turn the pick slightly backwards. Don't actually turn the pick backwards yourself, of course; just releasing some tension should be enough to cause this. The feelers should neatly hold all of the other pins in place while you push the mushroom or spool pin completely past the shear line and set the pin stack.

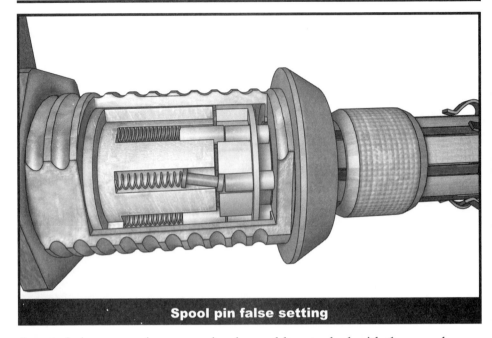

Spool pin false setting

Serrated pins are again an even harder problem to deal with than mushroom
or spool pins. Serrated pins can be found in place of both the key and
driver pins. The serrated pins, when properly installed, can produce a very
convincing false set. Pushing down on the serrated pin may not cause the
pick to counter-rotate much at all. For this reason, you will have to be very
sensitive to the most subtle movement of the pick. Loosen up on the turning
torque and push down on the pin stack you suspect of having the serrated
pin. As you push the feeler, you should feel the pick turning in the opposite
direction to the torque. Allow for counter-rotating to happen. Don't fight it
too much, but continue applying some torque. It is a very fine balance and
will require a lot of experience to get just right. Then, all of a sudden, you
should feel the pick rotate in the correct direction of the torque again. You
may have to repeat this rotation/counter-rotation a few times to move the
pin along the various serrations. It is important and incredibly difficult to
know which serration is the actual break between the key and driver pins.
The correct set will usually allow the pick to rotate forward a little bit more
than a serration would, but it's very difficult to notice this. Stop when you
reach this break between the pins; otherwise, you will push the key pin
below the shear line. Serrated pins are very difficult and many locksmiths
are unable to reliably pick them individually.

Another effective countermeasure is the *thin key pin*. With thin key pins, it is possible to push the driver pin below the shear line and set the pin stack, but then easily push the thin key pin below the shear line and relock the lock. When you encounter the thin key pin, you will feel very distinct feedback as you push down on the feeler. As you push down on the binding pin stack, you will feel a lot of constant resistance as the thicker driver pin is pushed, binding across the shear line and against the spring.

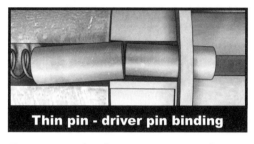

Thin pin - driver pin binding

Then, all of a sudden, your pick will slightly rotate. You may hear a click, and you will feel a lot less resistance. If you just keep pushing, you will quickly shove the key pin below the shear line.

Once you do that, you can only try to somehow pull the feeler back up. If you manage to pull the feeler up, you will allow the spring to push the driver pin up to the shear line again. It is best to practice, however, to stop pushing altogether as soon as you feel the indications that the pin stack has set.

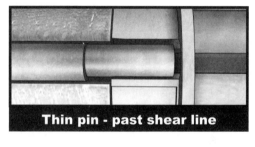

Thin pin - past shear line

In order to do this, you will have to carefully control how you push the feelers. It's best to try pushing the feelers a little distance at a time and avoid simply increasing pressure without being ready to stop the movement of the feeler.

Thin pin - properly set

Sometimes manufacturers may also include rounded or tapered pins. These can achieve the same effect of a thin pin, and can also slide and jam below the shear line. You can deal with these pins in the same manner as when they are in the traditional pin tumbler.

Rounded and Tapered Key Pins

Beveled pinholes are also starting to appear in tubular locks. Just as in the case of pin tumbler locks, bevels provide an effective security measure. Bevels are usually exactly above the shear line and may only be done for some of the holes for added confusion.

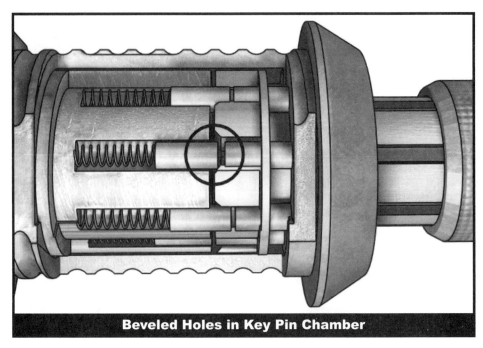

Beveled Holes in Key Pin Chamber

Bevels prolong the lock picking process and, thereby, make the locks more secure. When bevels are present, you might have to pick the same pin stack a couple of times. Imagine the pin stack that you are about to press down is binding. The tip of the driver pin would be resting on the bevel. As you press down the key and driver pins, the driver pin will slide downwards into the wider part of the bevel; that will allow the pick to turn a little bit. The turning of the lock, however, will ensure that another pin stack will now bind, and you will have to stop picking the current pin stack. If you don't stop pushing on the feeler, you risk sliding the key pin below the shear line, especially if the key pin is tapered, rounded, or thin. When you pick a beveled pin stack, you will first feel the resistance of the binding driver pin and the spring. Then all of a sudden, just as the lock turns ever so slightly, it will become much easier to push down the feeler. If you think that you pushed the feeler too far down, try to pull the feeler in a little bit and loosen the turning tension on the pick so that the spring can push the key pin above the shear line.

Improvised Tools

Most of the tubular locks have improved in quality as the years go by. However, there is always a market for cheaper low-security solutions; sometimes reputable companies just start abandoning good practice in a short-sighted search of profits. This means that some of the tubular locks that you encounter can be picked open with something as simple and cheap as a Bic pen. The real secret is that, although cheap, the Bic pen meets all the complex requirements of a rudimentary tubular pick.

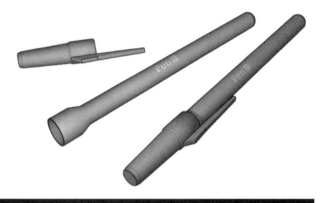

Enlarged pen for an improvised rake

To you, the lock picker, the important piece of the Bic pen is the body. You should remove the cap and the front of the pen that you write with, along with the back end of the pen. All that is left is the plastic cylinder that makes up the body of the pen. Try to slide the pen body into the lock to see if it fits easily. If the body is slightly smaller than the lock opening you are trying to pick, you may have to widen the tip of the body that will enter the lock. Widening the body can be accomplished by pushing slightly larger Philips screwdrivers into it, scraping the inside with knives, rotating scissor blades inside it, or using some other improvised technique. Constantly retry to fit the pen body into the lock.

This widening process is definitely not quick, and you would probably have a much easier time with a real rake, but sometimes you may only have a ballpoint pen handy. Once you can relatively easily slide the tip of the pen all the way in and out of the lock, you will find out how well the lock was really constructed. Push the pen in the lock and just jiggle it back, forth, sideways and around, while trying to apply some force against the tip. As you turn the cylinder, you may be able to open the lock. The idea is that, with some force and jiggling, you will be able to rake the lock as you did with a tubular rake pick by deforming the thinned-out walls of the tip into something that resembles a key. Once all the jiggling is complete and the body of the pen is deformed, your ad hoc pick will be able to open the lock with relative ease. Furthermore, your successive attempts to open the lock will involve much less force and jiggling because the approximate shape of the key will already be ready for use. If the pins are all cut to similar heights, this method can work much faster and more reliably. On the other hand, a well-manufactured lock, or one that has lots of variations in its key cuts, or several anti-rake and anti-pick countermeasures built-in will not be susceptible to this form of attack. In fact, this method will not work for most tubular locks.

If the opening on your lock isn't even close in size to the diameter of the pen and you still want to try this method, you can use different materials to get the job done. The material you choose needs to be deformable, but not too easy to bend out of shape. One easily-accessible material that can work on some

Cut material for improvised rake

locks is thin, multi-layered cardboard or plastic. Be creative: try various tubes, pens, or whatever else is lying around.

You should measure the tubular lock opening in order to see how much material you need. After you do this, cut out the appropriate amount of material. After you finish cutting, roll up your material so it fits snugly into the keyhole. Once you are finished constructing your tool, you should follow the same steps as with the pen body tool in order to open the lock.

Please remember that most tubular locks are well-designed and can't be picked with these rather primitive approaches. If you are in a situation where you don't have access to sophisticated tools and opening the lock right then is critical, then the improvised tools are much better than nothing at all.

6

Lever Locks

Lever Locks

The *lever tumbler lock* is an invention straight from the heart of old England. Lever tumbler locks are still used around the world, but especially in the United Kingdom. In the United States, you're likely to find them in the safety deposit vault at your local bank. Before these locks were invented, most people relied on warded lock, which offered alarmingly poor security. As society evolved, the need for more sophisticated physical security became evident. English royalty offered prizes to people who could invent more and more secure locks, as well as to those people who could expose the faults and deficiencies of these new locks.

Historical Lever Locks

Simple Lever Lock

The first lever lock invented was really quite simple. This design involved just one *lever*. The key would rotate and its blade would raise the lever, allowing the bolt to slide back into the lock housing. This lock mechanism only ensured that the bolt would remain locked out of the lock housing when the key was removed. When the key was inserted and rotated, it pushed the lever up while moving the bolt inward. This design could still be combined with wards to frustrate picking.

Picking these lever locks was rather easy until the day Robert Barron introduced a more complex lever lock. His version of the lever lock required the key to lift the lever to exactly the right height in order for the bolt to move. If the lever were raised too high or too low, it would prevent the bolt from moving.

In Barron's lever lock, the lever had a post that would move up and down a slot inside the bolt. As you can see, the lever would have to be raised to

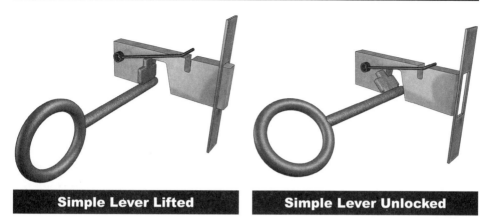

Simple Lever Lifted   **Simple Lever Unlocked**

just the right height to allow the bolt to move sideways. Only at this correct height was there an opening in the side of the slot where the post could fit through, allowing the bolt to slide sideways.

To make these locks more secure, the single lever was augmented with more levers side by side. They each had to be raised to the right height for the bolt to move. The groove on the bottom of each lever where the key blade and lever touch is called the *saddle*. The saddle was cut to match the key and lift the lever to the right distance. Each saddle could be made at different depths, allowing for a specific pattern of cuts in the key blade. This lock was such an improvement that it was considered pickproof for some time. Unfortunately, there was a major weakness in Barron's lever lock design. If the relative depths of each saddle were known, then it would not only be possible to compromise the lock once, but also to make a key that regularly opened the lock with ease. This left the locks vulnerable to impressioning.

It was possible to push a blank key tipped with wax against the levers. By looking at the depressions left in the wax, the shape of the saddle could be discerned, and thus, the approximate cut of the key. Lever tumbler locks had to evolve some more in order to remain in widespread use.

Barron's Lever Lock

How Lever Locks Work

Let's now look at the modern version of the lever lock design. As you can see in this illustration, the arrangement of the levers and bolt is somewhat different. It is now the levers which have slits in them, and the bolt that has the post. This *bolt post* must slide through the slit in order to lock or unlock this design. All the levers have the same depth saddle, which makes impressioning harder. Instead, they have the slits cut at different heights. When the key lifts the lever, it will be raised to the correct height allowing the bolt post to easily slide in and out of the lever.

Modern Lever Lock

Because all of the saddles are aligned and the same size, it is now impossible to gain any information about the key by pushing on all of the levers at the same time and impressioning the resulting shape. If you try to

Levers with different slits

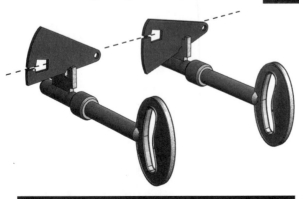

Key raises Levers and aligns slits

impression a modern lever lock by simply pushing up a blank key tipped with wax against the levers, then all of the levers will lift to exactly the same height. You would end up with flat depressions in the wax that do not mimic the key shape.

Sometimes there are as few as three levers. In more secure installations, there can be more then ten. Interestingly, some locks are designed so that the key is cut symmetrically. This is for the locks that can accept the key from either side of the lock. The levers are arranged so that it doesn't matter from which side the key is inserted.

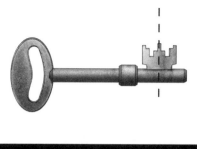

Symmetrical Key

We now have a basic understanding of how lever locks work, so let's take a closer look at the pieces that make up the lock. The lever is not quite as simple as we have just described.

Lever Spring

Pictured here is a typical lever that you might encounter. The round hole on the end of the lever is called the *pivot hole*. A pin inside the lock goes through that hole and acts as an axel around which the levers pivot or turn. All of the levers are installed on the same pin, so they all rotate around the same point. The long, thin, bent metal piece sticking out of the lever is a spring. In normal operation, as shown in the picture, the spring is bent and pushes against the body of the lock. Under the pressure of the spring, the lever turns around the pin in the pivot hole all the way down until it hits the bottom of the lock body. It rests there until a key lifts it up to open the lock. Take note of the chamber within this lever that the bolt post rests in when the lock is unlocked and the bolt has retracted into the lock body. This chamber is called the *rear trap*.

Some types of lever locks have two chambers in which a bolt post can reside. The rear trap houses the bolt post when the bolt is inside the lock, and the *front trap* contains the bolt post when the bolt is sticking out of the lock.

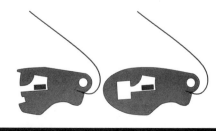

Levers with Bolt Post

Levers are tightly packed next to each other. This could cause problems if the levers touched each other. If the levers' large flat surfaces were pressed against each other, there would be too much friction between them. As a result, it would be difficult to lift one lever without disturbing the neighboring ones.

Spacers prevent one lever from disturbing its neighbors. Spacers themselves don't move at all. They each have a pivot hole. They don't have a spring and are always in contact with the bolt post. Since the spacers only have a slit cut into them that the post can travel along instead of a larger chamber, they don't rotate

Lever Spacer

around the pivot hole. The bolt post can easily slide along the slit without ever leaving it as it locks and unlocks. The key never comes into contact with the spacer itself, because the saddle in the spacer is cut deeper than the saddle on any lever.

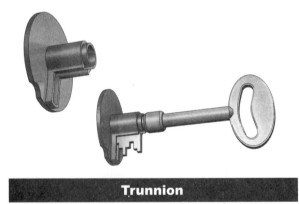

Trunnion

Another important piece of the lever lock is the *trunnion*. When you insert the key into the lock, it will not be confined inside a keyway as it would in a pin tumbler lock. Instead, the key will slip inside a metallic chamber that will turn along with the key.

The trunnion ensures that the key stays perpendicular to the levers throughout the turn. At the same time, the trunnion makes picking much harder by denying easy access to the levers. Picture, if you will, what the keyhole would look like when the lock is completely unlocked. Now picture what it would look like when the trunnion is half turned by someone trying to pick the lock.

Keyhole and Trunnion

As you can imagine, when the trunnion is half-turned, it is only possible to access the levers through the upper round part of the keyhole. Normally, the flat face of the trunnion cylinder has a notch that allows the key to enter. As the trunnion is rotated, this notch also rotates; only the round part of the keyhole remains open.

Round keys will only have the round stem of the key filling the hole in the trunnion. Some locks are designed for flat keys, however. These keys can be made with a special cut near the head of the key. This *throat cut* allows the key to rotate, once it is inside the keyhole, without interfering with the body of the lock. Everything from the tip of the key to the throat cut is cradled

Flat Lever Key

by the trunnion, while everything from the throat cut to the end of the handle is outside of the lock. The amount of material left on the key below the throat cut determines how much space is available for the tools that will enter and manipulate the lever lock. The spring forces inside the lever lock are relatively high, so it takes a significant amount of turning tension to open the lock with the key. If the key can't handle the repeated application of turning tension, it will break at its thinnest point. For this reason, the throat cut can't be so deep that it just leaves a small sliver of metal on the key. It also means that you will have a harder time picking the lock because the forces you need to apply to the levers are greater. Prison lever locks can be very large with very strong springs, making them a particular challenge.

This is why the trunnion greatly improves the operation and security of the lever lock. If the trunnion was simply allowed to rotate freely, then it would be possible for it to rotate when the key wasn't inside the lock. A half-rotated trunnion would prevent the key from entering the keyway just as it prevents your picking tools from using the entire space of the keyway. Because of this, various methods are used to prevent the trunnion from easily rotating without the key.

One solution is the use of a spring that can slide in and out of a groove in the trunnion. You should keep in mind that this is yet another force that must be overcome when turning the key.

Now let's put all the pieces of the puzzle together and take a look at how the various pieces of the lock fit together:

Trunnion and Spring in Casing

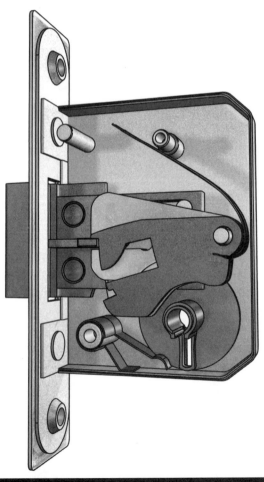

Lever Lock - locked

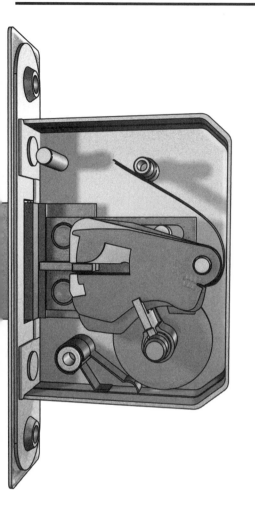

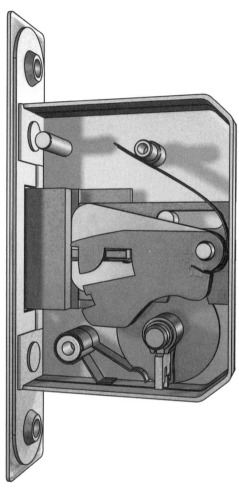

Lever Lock - with Key unlocking it

Picking Lever Locks

At this point, you should have a good grasp of how the lever lock works, and how the pieces of the lever lock act in unison to make a complete whole. You are now well-prepared to study the picking methods that can defeat this lock. The picks that you will use are vaguely familiar to the picks that you used for opening pin tumbler locks.

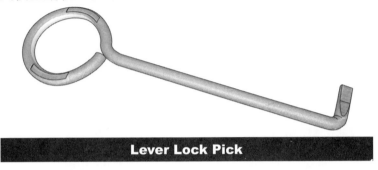

Lever Lock Pick

Here's an example pick. In this case, the handle is a round hoop. That's because you will not only push the pick up and down, but also rotate it with some significant force as well. Lever lock picks can be found in a wide assortment of shapes. The tip of the pick comes in a variety of different heights in order to accommodate various lever lock shapes and sizes. The picks themselves also vary in size and thickness.

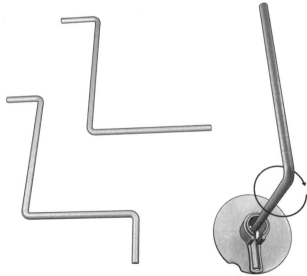

Lever Torque Wrenches

The second tool that you will use should be very familiar by now. It is the torque wrench. This tool is always used in unison with the pick. The torque wrench has a small tip that rotates the trunnion. Sometimes both ends of the wrench have a tip, usually of different sizes, in order to accommodate different locks. In order to provide enough operating room for the pick, the torque wrench should be pushed all the way to the back of the trunnion.

If your lock can be opened from both sides, make sure that your torque wrench isn't pushed so far into the lock that it is pushing the doorframe when you try to apply turning tension. You should insert the torque wrench into the lock first, followed by the pick. You can then apply a little bit of turning tension to the torque wrench, and the trunnion will begin to rotate. Once the trunnion rotates far enough that the torque wrench can't be pushed out of the other side of the lock, you should push the torque wrench further into the lock until it can't be pushed any further. Then, turn the tension wrench until the trunnion won't allow it to rotate any further. The reason you won't be able to turn it any more is because rotating the trunnion moves the bolt in and the bolt post will come into contact with one of the levers.

Like when picking other tumbler lock designs, you are attempting to exploit slight variations in the sizes of the manufactured mechanical parts. If the levers were manufactured to exactly the same size, then the bolt post would contact all of them at exactly the same time. In the real world it will contact one of them more forcefully than the rest. This allows you to pick one lever at a time. Use your pick to push up on the levers until you find the lever that resists the most. You've now found the first binding lever. Push this lever up until the bolt post starts to enter the rear trap of that lever. You will hear or feel a slight click or movement, and your torque wrench will slightly rotate when the bolt post begins to enter the back trap. It will be very subtle, though, because soon another lever will bind and prevent the post from moving further. You will have to repeat this process for each lever. Keep in mind that the bolt post has already entered the slit of the set lever, so you don't have to worry about accidentally moving and unsetting it as long as you maintain enough tension on the torque wrench. Too much tension is also a problem, though, since that would cause the post to bind strongly with multiple levers.

Before you try to pick a lever lock that is already installed inside a door or other installation, it helps to practice on a common door lock that is not yet installed. Many lever locks have a small window in the body of the lock. This window allows you to see how the levers move up and when the bolt post enters the back trap. It can be a very helpful learning aid as you first try to pick lever locks.

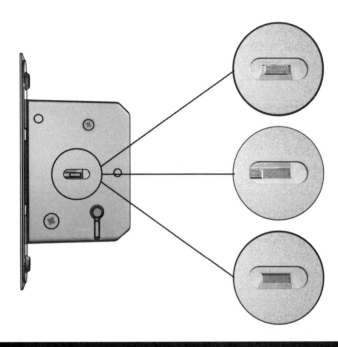

Example Lever Lock Window

You will be able to see which levers are still unpicked and which ones are already set. While it is a great training aid, don't get accustomed to the luxury of looking at the insides of a lock while you are picking it. Later on, you should probably tape over the window so that you can't rely on your vision to pick the lock.

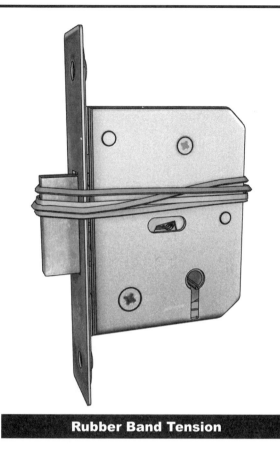

Rubber Band Tension

It can be cumbersome to hold the lock in your hand while separately manipulating the torque wrench and the pick. To make your first few picking attempts easier, you can try using some strong rubber bands to put pressure on the bolt instead of the torque wrench. Simply wrap strong rubber bands around the lock so that they push the bolt into the lock. Now you will only have to hold the lock and manipulate the pick without bothering with the torque wrench. You can use this technique in the very beginning, but after a few successful attempts, you should remove the rubber bands and work with the torque wrench instead. This will only work on some locks, but it can be a useful training aid when it does.

High Security Levers

Counter-picking measures have been integrated into many of the lever locks sold today. One of the most common countermeasures is the use of *false notches* in the lever. These serve to trap the bolt post with a false setting.

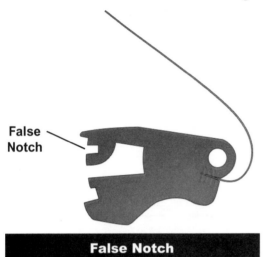

False Notch

False Notch

As you can see, if the bolt post is being pushed against this lever while the lever is being lifted, then the bolt post will first slide into the upper false notch. As long as there is a constant force on the bolt post, it will be trapped in this false notch. This design is reminiscent of the spool pin from the pin tumbler lock. You can deal with it in a similar manner. Release tension to let the bolt post out of the notch. Of course, this might mean that other levers will unset themselves as you release tension. What makes this particularly difficult is that when you first set it, the false notch will feel exactly the same as the real thing. You won't know until later, when the bolt post hits the end of the short notch, that something is amiss. A single lever might have many false notches. You will have to experiment with the levers to find out which ones have multiple notches and try different combinations until you find the right one.

Some designs take this idea even further and actually have a completely serrated edge of the lever, as well as a modified bolt post that can easily catch on the lever. This design is reminiscent of the serrated pin design from the high-security pin tumbler lock.

To make things even harder, these high-security locks are made with very tight tolerances. The bolt post might catch on the edge of the lever, even if it is just one one-thousandth of an inch higher or lower than the proper height to which the key would lift. Every lever in the lock might contain both serrations and false notches, making this a very effective counter-picking measure. Safety deposit boxes in banks often contain up to 14 of these high-security levers. Give one of these high-security lever locks a try, and you will see that they are, indeed, very resistant to picking.

You may very well still be able to defeat inferior implementations of these locks with some luck and determination. A lever can often have as little as one false trap. If the bolt post is trapped inside a false trap, it will be very difficult to determine which lever has trapped the post. With poorly-made lever locks that don't have tight manufacturing tolerances, you may be able to apply some torque to your wrench and feel which lever is binding. Thus, you can determine

Serrated Lever

which lever caught the bolt post in its false notch trap. In order to sense the difference in binding strength, you have to be very skilled. The lever that is binding will not be able to move at all, while the other levers that are properly set will only move very slightly. Once you find the appropriate lever, you can loosen some tension and try to pick that lever again into a different position which is, hopefully, the real trap. Remember, loosening the tension may lead to other levers springing down as well. You may have to repeat this cycle several times. If it becomes cumbersome to constantly repick the same levers, you can try to remember at which heights the various levers have notches. That way you will have an easier time starting over each time while looking for the right combination of notches.

You will know that you are dealing with serrated levers if picking a lever causes your torque wrench to counter-rotate. You will know that a lever is set if pushing on it while applying torque to the wrench doesn't cause the wrench to counterrotate. You can loosen some torque and manipulate the lever in hopes that it will set. Unfortunately, in high-security locks, there are many correctly-set levers that can fall once you loosen the tension. It is also incredibly easy to push the lever too high past the entrance of the notch until it catches on the next serration. Unless you are dealing with a poor-quality lever lock, these are very difficult to pick. Of course, most lever locks with serrated levers are not of poor quality.

Master Keying Lever Locks

Just like pin tumblers, lever locks can be deployed with master key arrangements. This means that two different keys will open the same lock. One of those keys usually also opens many different locks. There are two simple methods to achieve this. First, there could be two back traps in the same lever. In this case the two keys are cut at two very different heights. A key could lift the lever to the height of either one of the two true notches. Either one will allow the bolt post to move inwards and unlock.

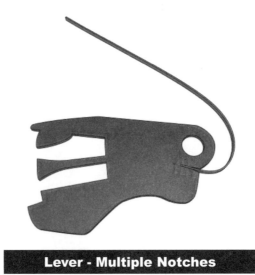

Lever - Multiple Notches

When the key cuts aren't drastically different between the two keys, it is possible to simply enlarge the single opening of a single notch into the back trap. This allows two keys with slightly different cuts to each set the lever at an acceptable height.

Lever - Enlarged Notch

Master keying provides the useful capabilities of master keys. Some restricted individuals could get keys that only work a single door, while the manager could have a single master key that works on all of the doors. Adding either of these lever designs, however, makes lock picking much easier. The chances of pushing the bolt post into a true notch is higher if there are more of them or if they are bigger. In large institutions that deploy master key schemes which require multiple levers with multiple notches, your job gets even easier. Even if master keys are needed, security is still a concern. For this reason, many of these levers will also have some of the counter-picking measures we discussed earlier. This may make them even harder to open than a regular lever lock.

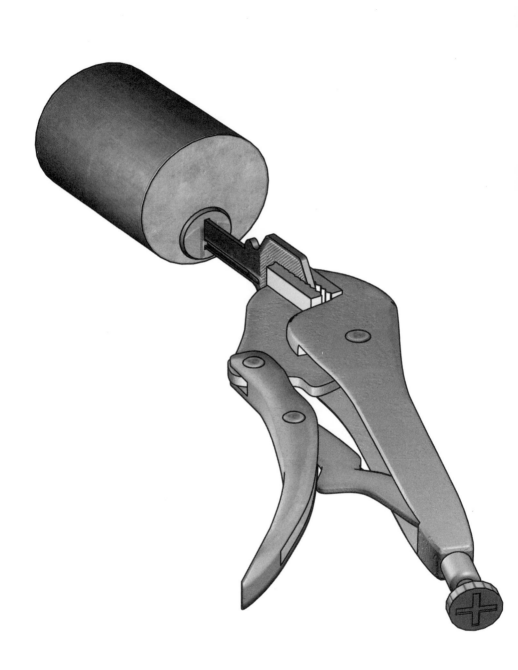

7

Impressioning
Tumblers

Impressioning

Tumblers

Picking a pin or wafer tumbler lock usually involves using specialized or improvised tools to manipulate the pins. There is another approach that uses an actual key instead. With this method you will end up with a working key that will open the lock. It might not be the prettiest key, but that's not the point. Welcome to the technique of *impressioning*. There are some drawbacks, of course. It may take some significant time and it definitely requires the right touch. Since you will be making an actual key, it is also a lot harder to start over than you may be used to with traditional picking or raking techniques.

Impressioning is a very powerful technique exactly because it creates an actual key for the lock that you are trying to open. The theory behind impressioning is fairly simple to understand. In practice, however, it is a very delicate art to master. If you dedicate yourself to this skill, you will probably be able to open locks with very few pin stacks or wafers. Impressioning keys for house or car locks is much more difficult since there are so many ways to make a mistake. It is only through extensive, hands-on experience that you can reliably achieve success. As a warning, gaining this experience can be both difficult and expensive. Instead of using picks and a torque wrench as your tools, you are going to make an actual key. That also means every failed attempt is a wasted key. Every impressioning attempt also slightly deforms the lock and makes it harder to impression that lock again. You may find it easier to pick the lock, and then remove and disassemble it from the inside in order to find the appropriate key cut. Even though there may often be a better way to open the lock, impressioning does have a place, especially on lower-security desk and file locks that only have one or two pins.

In order to impression, you will need only two or three simple tools and a blank key to start with. The appropriate blank will slide in and out of the keyhole with ease. It should completely fill the keyhole, and it shouldn't be possible to wiggle it around too much once it is inserted into the lock.

For the tools, you will need a file to make grooves in the key and prepare it for impressioning. After this section, you will be familiar with what kind of filing is required for impressioning; this allows you to select the file that best suits your metalworking style and lock type. A vice-grip, pliers, or some tool that can grab on to the key and provide good leverage will come in handy. Lastly, a magnifying glass to clearly see the marks on the key is often a big help. It is actually quite possible to impression a key without a magnifying glass if you have good eyesight, but it is always a good idea to make your job as easy as possible.

Magnifying Glass

Files

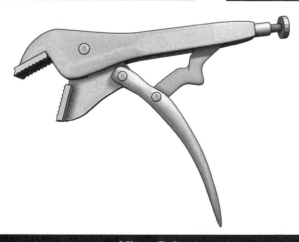

Vice-Grip

Blank Preparation

As you may have guessed, the first step is to get the appropriate blanks for your lock. If it is a common lock, then they should be readily available from an appropriate supplier. It helps to have a few extra spares available for the inevitable mistakes. If you are dealing with a more specialized lock for which blanks are not sold, then improvisation is the key.

Once you have the blanks, you will have to prepare them for impressioning. This blank will hopefully become your working key, but first we have to get it ready. There are two effective ways to prepare the blanks. One method simply smoothes out the top of the key so there are no distinguishable marks on it. Remember, this is where it comes into contact with the bottom pins on a pin tumbler lock. When you smooth out that surface, be careful not to file down too much. If you file too far down, and one of the pin stacks needed a completely uncut key depth, then you have just succeeded in ruining your first blank. Don't worry, this will happen a lot when you're first learning. If you went on and tried to use this blank, your impressioning attempt will fail. Filing down the key at that location all the way to the maximum depth will do nothing. Therefore, if the key still has slight marks after a light initial filing, just inspect it carefully and commit the marks to memory. Then disregard these marks later when you are looking for the marks left by the bottom pins. We will get to what these marks look like soon.

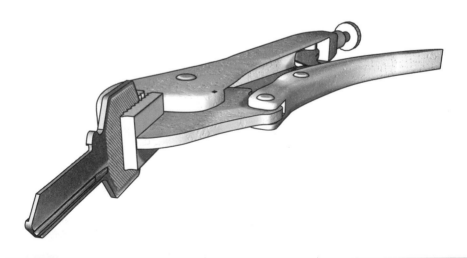

Blank with a smooth flat surface

An alternative way to prepare the key blank for impressioning is to file the top of the key into a somewhat sharp knife-edge. Don't try to make your blank sharp enough to cut something. Rather, just shape the top of the key into a pointed tip. In other words, instead of a flat top, file away one side of the blank to a slope from the middle of the blade down, at a 40 to 50 degree angle. File down on the other side as well to produce the pointed edge for the blade on the blank key. If you decide to file both sides of the blade, you should be especially careful that you don't file away the top of the key in some places. If a part of the top of the key is filed away below the point a pin stack requires, you will have the same problem as the previous preparation method, and have ruined another blank. Remember to start with plenty of spares while you're learning.

This second style of blank preparation is popular because the pins or wafers can leave stronger, more recognizable marks. Knife-edge filing involves some more skill, though, since all the grooves for the pin stacks that need to be made as you impression this lock will also have to be filed at an angle. For your first attempts, before you've gained much experience with where to file and how much, it's probably best to start with the simpler smoothing method. When you get accustomed to precise filing, then knife-edge blanks have a clear advantage of providing more distinct marks to follow.

Many also prefer to coat the blank surface with a layer of carbon by holding it above a lit candle. This soot coating can help to distinguish marks, but the process should be repeated for each impression attempt. This is described in more detail in Chapter 1. However, the wax coating mentioned will not work for tumbler impressioning.

Blanks filed smooth or with an edge

Lock Impressioning

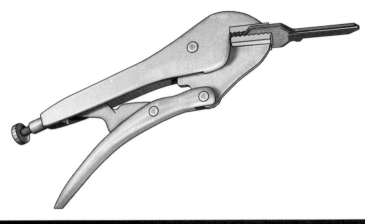

Grip the blank firmly with the vice-grip

Impressioning is all about reading the lock by putting marks on the blank, reading those marks, and filing the blank to make a working key. So, now that your blank key is ready for impressioning, it's time to insert it into

the lock and make some of those marks. Grab a vice-grip and tightly clamp the key at the handle. Vice-Grips can hold very tightly and will probably mark up your key's handle with teeth marks. Those aren't the marks we are interested in. Insert the key straight into the lock. Be careful not to apply any sideways pressure to the key while you are inserting it into the keyway.

Insert blank carefully

Next, turn the key to one side as far as you can. Do not apply a lot of torque when you meet resistance. Applying extra torque will not leave the right kind of marks on the key. In order to make the right marks, you will have to move the key up and down once it is fully turned to one side.

When the key is fully turned to one side and held with appropriate pressure, then one of the pins will bind while the others will still be able to move up and down. Refer back to the chapter on how pin tumblers work and how

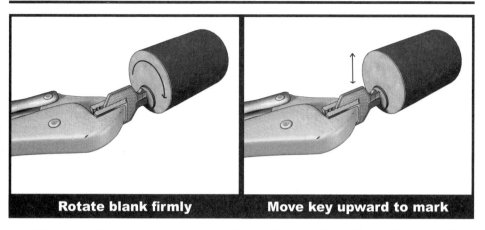

Rotate blank firmly | Move key upward to mark

to pick them if you're not clear on how this works. If you keep the key turned and then move it up and down, you will press it against the pin that is binding. Moving it up and down on this pin that is sticking should mark the blank at the spot of the binding pin stack. While you are at it, you can turn the key to the other side and do the same thing.

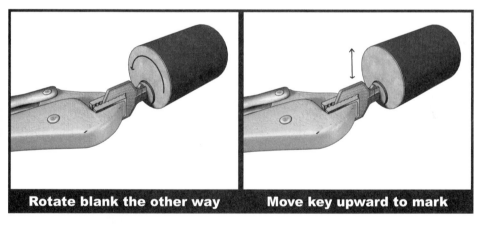

Rotate blank the other way | Move key upward to mark

Most likely, a different pin will bind, and moving it up and down will leave a mark for this second pin.

After turning the key both ways and moving it up and down on each side, you can pull the key out of the lock. As you insert the key and take it out, always be careful to not mark the blade too much more. Now take a close look at the key. As you might expect, different marks will be left on the key, depending on whether the lock is a pin tumbler or wafer design. Pin tumblers will leave mostly round marks, while wafers leave stripes on the key.

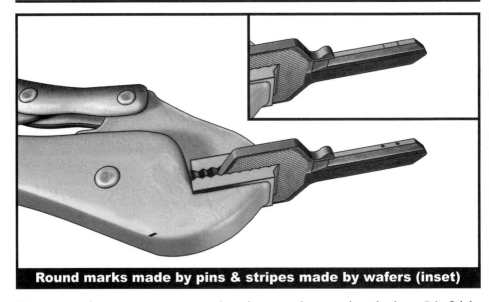

Round marks made by pins & stripes made by wafers (inset)

You may only see one or two marks when you impression the key. It's fairly evident then, that you need to file at those locations. However, you may often encounter faint marks on the key. These may be marks left by pins or simply by lock irregularities. Pin stacks that need very deep key cuts will also initially leave faint marks. These marks will get stronger as the blank is filed down at that location. When filed to the correct depth, these marks will disappear. If you continue filing down, then the marks will appear again. It is also likely there will be long scratches on the blade as the pins slide against it while the key is being inserted or removed. It is best to ignore these long scratches and any faint marks altogether. Concentrate solely on the most prominent marks on the key where the pins should be.

When you find the spots that have the most pronounced marks, you can file down the key at these locations. These are the locations where the bottom pins were binding. That means that the bottom pin is crossing the shear line and the notch needs to be deeper to allow the pin stack to lower just the right amount and separate. When filing the key you should keep several things in mind. First, don't file down too deeply. If you do so, you risk the possibility that

File slightly at marks

you will miss the appropriate key depth and will have to start all over again. Second, always make it easy for the pins to slide in and out of the groove that you are cutting. If the sides of the groove are too steep, it is possible that the pins could get stuck inside the groove. This could even mean you wouldn't be able to remove the key from the lock.

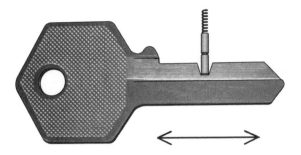

Notches cut too steep might trap pin and hold key in lock

Third, try to leave a polished surface on which another mark can be made. If you are filing the key in the knife-edge fashion, remember to keep the filing cuts tilted.

When you first start filing, make a cut with the sharp end of a file. Don't worry about the sloped sides. You first need to make sure that you're filing at the right place. Since the mark will disappear as soon as you start filing, you should make sure to leave an indentation at the exact place that the mark was left. This indentation should be narrow and exactly on the mark. Next you can use your file to create the slopes which allow the pin stacks to slide up and down as the key is inserted.

There are files that have a square or rectangular cross-section. These will allow you to easily make slopes at a 45-degree angle. Others have only a thin cross-section. In that case, you will have to tilt the file in both directions in order to create the slope. If you are using a completely round file, you need to exert sideways pressure in order to create the slopes.

Since you only filed the key down in a couple of locations by slight amounts, you are still far from having a working key. This process of inserting the key, turning it, moving it up and down to mark it, and filing the marks down will have to be repeated many times. Each time you file, it should only

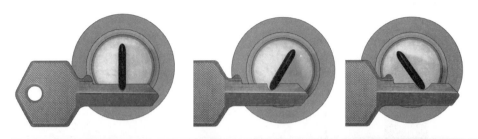

File straight, then create the slopes

be by a slight amount: maybe even only a few strokes with the file. As you keep impressioning and filing down one position, the marks will get stronger and stronger, until all of a sudden, they disappear. As soon as it no longer yields a mark, don't file down on that position anymore. If you continue filing down, or if you accidentally file down too much, the marks will appear again. This happens because the upper pin is now binding and forcing the lower pin to leave a mark. It is always better to err by not filing the groove deep enough. You can always impression and file down some more; it's a lot harder to start over again. Since you should only file down slightly more in each step, you can imagine that impressioning might take quite a while. The quality and tolerances of the lock will determine how exact you have to be with your cuts.

The reason that only certain pin stacks cause marks is because marks are caused by binding pins. Remember from the pin tumblers chapter, we discussed how certain pin stacks will have the top pins bind first when you apply torque. In this case, the blank pushes up all of the pin stacks, so it is the bottom pins that bind. The pin stacks that bind will be held firmly in place and will cause marks as the key moves against them. The other pins that don't bind will jiggle freely with the key and leave no mark. Once you have filed a notch at that location to the correct depth, then the bottom pin will no longer bind when torque is applied. This means that no mark is created, letting you know it is filed to the correct depth. When that happens, some other bottom pin might start to bind, causing a mark to be made when the key is moved against it. Remember that just because there is no mark at a pin location, it does not mean the notch is at the correct depth. It might just mean that another pin stack is binding. When that pin stack is filed correctly, other stacks can start to bind and cause marks. Now a word of caution: if you file a notch too deeply, the top pin will move past the shear line and also bind when torque is applied. That means that a mark will be made again. So, you will get a mark if the notch is either too deep or too shallow. Unfortunately, the mark will look the same in both cases. That is why it is so important to only file a small amount so that you do not accidentally file past the correct depth and miss it.

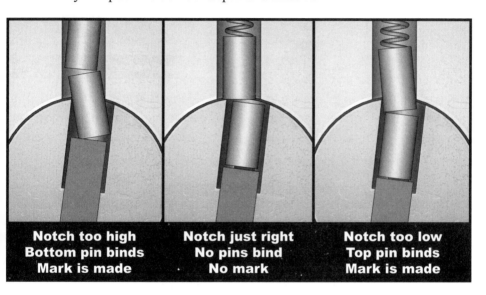

Notch too high	Notch just right	Notch too low
Bottom pin binds	No pins bind	Top pin binds
Mark is made	No mark	Mark is made

The same is also true for wafer tumblers. Marks will be made if the wafer raised too much or not enough. They are caused when the part of the wafer that protrudes out of the lock core binds against the lock hull. They can either be protruding out of the top or the bottom of the lock core. So again, it is critical to file just slightly so that you do not miss the right depth when the wafer is at just the right height: when it does not protrude out of the core, does not bind, and thus does not produce a mark. Experience will help you to know how much you can safely file each time. Since pins and wafers are usually made to a set of standard sizes, it is safe to file the notch from one depth to another. However, when you first start, it is best to be careful and only file slightly to avoid wasting blanks and starting over again.

As you repeatedly impression the key, you may find that the mark doesn't appear exactly at the lowest point of the groove. In that case, your notch might not be at the right spot and you will have to expand the groove sideways. When doing this be, careful to not accidentally make the groove deeper. Make sure that as you are filing, pressure is applied only to the side of the groove that needs to be moved.

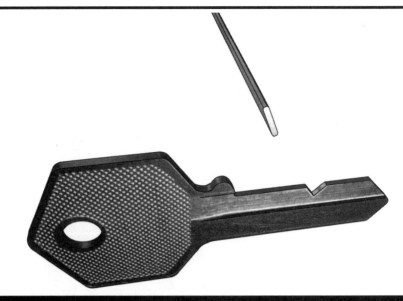

Mark on side of groove

Always concentrate on the strongest mark. You may be left with several faint marks on the key and still be able to open the lock. However, it is also possible that there are only a few faint marks left and the key refuses to open the lock. Some of those faint marks may simply occur because of lock imperfections, but others may reveal positions of very deep cuts in the key. It helps to polish the key at those locations and impression the key again. If you see a mark again, that increases the possibility that this indeed was a valid mark. Before you start filing the groove at that position, you may want to record the depth and location of existing grooves with a caliper. This makes it easier to recreate the key to this point so you don't have to start completely over again. Or you can just continue with another blank and file it to the same depths right away. If you are dealing with a lock that has more than two pins, one of the easiest ways to eliminate false marks is to check if they align with the spacing pattern of the marks that you already filed. The pin stacks are almost always arranged at regular intervals. Since the distance between any two neighboring pin stacks is the same, the marks that are left on the key should be consistent with that spacing. You can use a regular pick to count how many pin stacks there are in the lock. Once you have at least two grooves and know their locations, it becomes possible to eliminate some false marks based on where they are located. This principle is especially helpful when you attempt to impression a lock with many pins.

Like when picking a tumbler lock, it is important to remember to not put too much torque on the key while impressioning. Applying too much torque will cause too many pin stacks to bind. Constantly doing so will also cause the base of the bow to weaken; it may even snap off the key. Other than providing an excuse to practice with your broken key extractor, this is frustrating. Still, you should always keep a broken key extractor tool handy while impressioning, just in case. Also watch out for any cracks that start to appear at the base of the bow. If you notice any cracks on the key you are working with, you can duplicate the key's shape on a new blank before it breaks.

At some point when you try to impression the key again, it should actually succeed in opening the lock. When this happens, congratulations! You have just impressioned a key for your lock. The working key can be used by itself, or you can decode the pin depths from it with a measuring device and produce a proper key with a key-cutting device.

Impressioning Example

Following is a sample sequence of key cuts and impressioning marks that can demonstrate a typical attempt to impression a key. This example omits many steps that are the same and repeat filing at the same location just slightly deeper.

1

Choose a blank that fits exactly into the keyhole. It needs to be the correct length and shape so that it completely fits the keyway.

2

Polish the top of the blank with a file. Don't file down too deeply: just enough to smooth out imperfections on the surface of the top of the key.

3

Insert and impression the key against the pins. In this example, three marks appear on the blank key surface. The strongest mark is closest to the bow of the key, so start to file down at that location.

4

Make a groove at the location of the mark. The sides of the groove should not be too steep, and the groove itself should not be too deep. Polish the surface of the groove so that further marks at that location will be noticeable.

5

Impression the key and inspect it carefully again. A larger, stronger mark is left in the middle of the groove. This mark is strong enough that it may be the last mark seen at this location.

6

Make the groove at the marked location slightly deeper and wider. This process of impressioning and filing should be repeated many times.

7

Impression the key again. The mark in the groove is no longer noticeable. Instead, a strong mark further towards the tip of the key can be seen.

8

File a groove at the location where the mark was left. Repeat the process of impressioning and filing several times.

9

After another impressioning, a very strong mark is left on the side of the wall of the second groove. The mark is strong enough to imply that we are very close to the correct depth.

10

Do not make this groove deeper. Instead, widen the existing groove. Widening the groove lowers the depth of the key under the new mark without increasing the maximum depth of the whole groove.

11

After another impressioning of the lock, only two faint marks remain on the key, but the lock won't open. One of the faint marks, however, is right in the middle of the two grooves. Since pins are regularly spaced, this means that the middle mark is likely to be a real one.

12

File a shallow groove under the middle mark. Repeat impressioning and filing several times.

13

Impression the key again. A stronger mark on the key in the middle groove is apparent. Continue to file slightly deeper.

14

Widen and deepen the pin groove. Polish the key so that marks are more noticeable on its surface.

15

Impression the key again. A strong mark is in the middle groove. Since this mark is strong, be careful not to file too deeply.

16

After making a slightly deeper and wider groove, polish the key to prepare it for impressioning.

17

While attempting to impression the key, the lock actually opens. When the key is removed, however, there is still one faint mark left on it from the very first impression. This is a false mark and there is no need to be concerned.

8

Combination Locks

Combination Locks

Combination locks are convenient because they don't require keys to operate. That means one less thing for the user to lose or forget. They are also valuable for institutions that would otherwise have to manage vast numbers of keys and matching locks. Furthermore, all of the combinations can be easily kept on file and changed as locks are reassigned to new users. The combination can also be shared for guest access and then changed for increased security. Combination locks can be found everywhere from the inexpensive gym padlock to the high-security safe or bank vault. Because they cannot be picked like a lock with a key, a high-quality combination lock provides very good security.

How Combination Locks Work

The easiest way to open these locks is to simply discover the combination, often written down somewhere, or ask the right person. In lieu of this, you will have to defeat the lock itself. In order to understand how these locks can be compromised, it helps to first understand how they operate. Let's take a look at a very simplified combination lock example modeled after a combination padlock.

One Wheel

Notice the moving parts in this lock. In this picture, the wheel, bolt, lever, and shackle are essential for the lock. There is a hole in the center of the *wheel*. An axel goes through this hole, allowing the wheel to rotate. The *bolt* and *lever* also rotate around a pin and are spring-loaded. You'll notice that this lock is designed so that the bolt is normally pushed into a notch in the shackle. This keeps the padlock locked by holding the shackle in place and preventing the shackle from moving out of the lock body. When you pull on the shackle, it pushes the bolt and lever against the wheel. With the wheel in place, it prevents the lever from moving, which keeps the bolt firmly in the shackle and the padlock locked. If this wheel is rotated to just the right position, then a *wheel notch* in the wheel, called a *gate*, will line up with the lever and allow the lever and bolt to rotate into it. This frees the shackle and allows it to pop open.

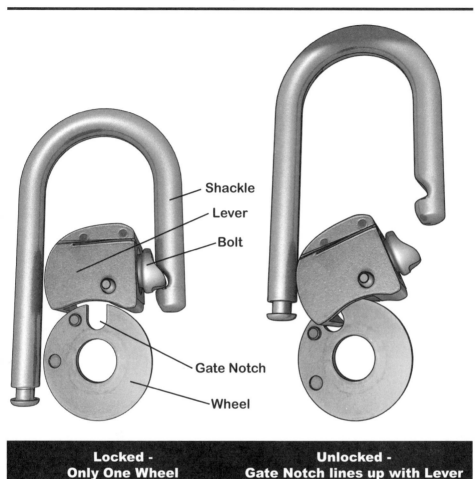

Shackle

Lever

Bolt

Gate Notch

Wheel

Locked -
Only One Wheel

Unlocked -
Gate Notch lines up with Lever

Only when the wheel is rotated to the correct position will the lock open. Imagine a faceplate attached to this wheel with numbers printed on it. To open the lock, you would turn the wheel to the correct number. We now have a simple, working combination lock, though with just one number in the combination.

Obviously, this example combination lock would be trivial to crack. Just rotate the wheel while pulling up on the shackle. Pulling on the shackle will push the lever against the wheel. Do this and rotate the wheel until the wheel notch lines up with the lever. When this happens, the lever will be pushed into the wheel notch and the lock will open. As you can see, this lock needs some improvements.

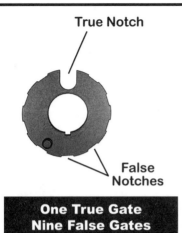

True Notch

False Notches

One True Gate Nine False Gates

For this reason, the wheels are actually more complex than the smooth wheels previously described in our example. If the wheel was smooth, except for the single notch cut into it, then it would be very easy to find out the correct combination for the lock. Manufacturers prevent this by giving the front wheel a special design. The front wheel still has only one true notch, also called a true gate, but it also has many other false notches. These prevent the faceplate from rotating if the lever is pushed into the wheel as described earlier. This modification makes it much more difficult to figure out the combination by lifting on the shackle and rotating the wheel. Many common locks come with 9 to 11 false notches and a single correct one, but some inexpensive locks are built with only one specially-designed false notch in addition to the correct one.

Lever stuck in False Notch   **Lever rotates into True Notch**

At this point, you might wonder how the lever, which contains the bolt, doesn't get stuck in one of these notches while the faceplate and front wheel are being rotated. The answer is that as long as we don't pull on the shackle, the lever is held away from all of the wheels. There is a spring attached to the lever that rotates it up and away from the wheels. ·

Lever
Spring

Lever Spring holds Lever away from Wheels

Cracking this one wheel combination lock, even with false notches, would still be very easy: just try each notch. Therefore, combination locks are never made with just one wheel. To make it more difficult, more wheels are added. In fact, combination locks have as many disks as there are numbers in the combination. Most common combination locks have three numbers and three wheels. Each wheel has a notch. This means that they all have to be positioned correctly to allow the lever to rotate and free the shackle. The front wheel is usually connected directly to the rotating faceplate of the lock, with numbers printed along the circumference of its face.

Even with multiple wheels, you need the false notches. Otherwise you could just pull up on the shackle or on the bolt while turning the wheel. This would force the lever to scrape along the wheels as they turned. It would be easy to feel when the lever would scrape on the gate, giving away a piece of the combination. The false notches are usually only on the front wheel and the "teeth" of the wheel extend past the other wheels, causing the lever to get stuck if pressure is applied while the wheel is being rotated.

Two Wheels

Now let's make things a little more complicated by adding a second wheel.

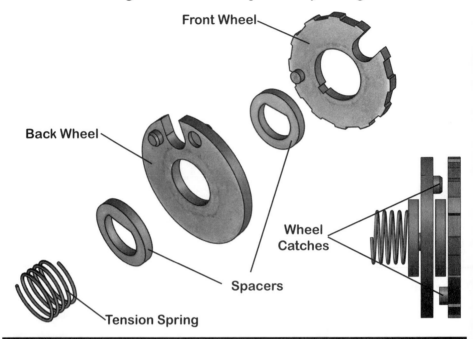

Combination Lock Parts - Only Two Wheels

The wheels are spaced slightly away from each other with *spacers*. These washers prevent the wheels from actually touching or disturbing their neighbors. The wheels and spacers are often held together by a wheel spring. Wheels rotate around a pin that goes through all of their center holes, while the spacers are designed to stay in place. The wheel spring also helps by providing some friction between the spacers and wheels, which holds the wheels in place when they are turned to the correct location. The reason spacers are necessary is because we don't want the rotation of one wheel to also rotate its neighboring wheel. The pin and spacers are specifically designed so that the pin is stationary and attached to the body of the lock. The spacers, once slid onto the pin, can't rotate. This prevents any transfer of rotation from one wheel onto another wheel.

Spacer does not rotate

What we have described so far are simple wheels where the user could rotate the faceplate and front wheel all day without moving the back wheel. To make the lock work, the wheels have *wheel catches*. Wheel catches are small protrusions on the sides of the wheels that face each other. When these protrusions line up, they make contact; any further turning of the front wheel will also turn the back wheel through the contacting wheel catches.

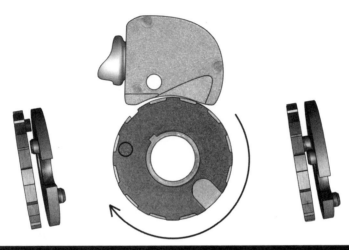

Reset lock by rotating several times to engage Wheel Catches

When approaching a lock, the wheel catches might not be in contact. However, if you rotate the front wheel clockwise for one full rotation, then its wheel catch is guaranteed to meet the catch of the next wheel. Since combination locks usually have three wheels, you usually have to turn the faceplate twice when you first start. This ensures that all of the wheel catches are touching. When all catches are touching, spinning the faceplate will spin all of the wheels. This is why the instructions for these locks always state to turn the faceplate two rotations clockwise before setting it to the first combination number.

Once you have reset the wheels, you can turn the faceplate to the first number. When you set the first number, the back wheel will be in its correct position. The back wheel should have its notch lining up with the bolt lever at this point. The lock still won't open, though, because the front wheel's notch does not line up.

Now you just have to turn the front wheel so it is in its correct position. If you kept rotating the front wheel clockwise, it would continue to move the back wheel out of position. But if you rotate the front wheel in the opposite direction, the wheel catch will disengage and leave the back wheel in place

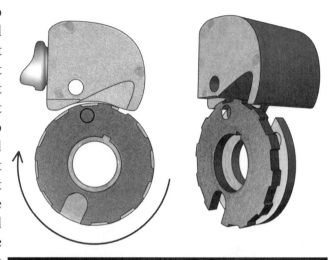

Back Wheel Set

undisturbed. It is important that you do not rotate the front wheel back more than one full rotation or the wheel catch will reengage on the other side. Just turn the wheel back to the correct second number; now both wheels should have their notches line up with the lever, allowing you to open the lock!

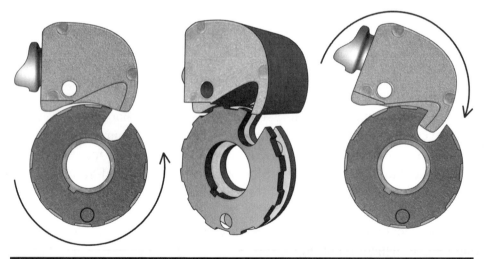

Both Wheels Set   **Lock Opens!**

Three Wheels

Most combination locks have three wheels to make them more secure. Let's add a third wheel to our example and see what it looks like:

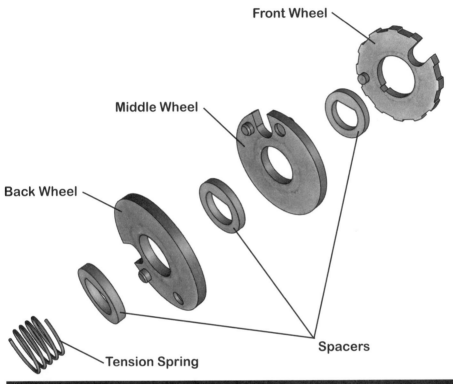

Combination Lock Parts - Three Wheels

When opening combination locks with three wheels, you still begin by rotating clockwise until all wheel catches are engaged. This means that you will have to rotate around once in order to make sure that the front wheel is catching the middle wheel, and then rotate once more to make sure that the middle wheel is catching the back wheel. You then continue to rotate clockwise until the first number, at which point the back wheel's notch will be lined up with the lever. The first number and the first wheel are now done. You next

**Reset Wheels -
All Wheel Catches Engaged**

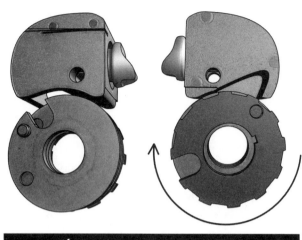

1ˢᵗ Number - Rear Wheel Set

need to set the middle wheel. The middle wheel must be moved by the wheel catch on the front wheel, which is attached to the faceplate. If you continued rotating the dial clockwise, the back wheel would continue to spin and move out of position. Therefore, you now need to rotate one full revolution counterclockwise in order for the wheel catch of the front wheel to engage with the other side of the wheel catch of the middle wheel. Now you can move the middle wheel counterclockwise to the appropriate amount in order to spin it into the correct position, where its notch also lines up with the lever. This is why the instructions for these locks always state that once you set the first number, you then need to turn the faceplate one full revolution counterclockwise before turning it to the second number. At this point, the back and middle wheels are set in position, and

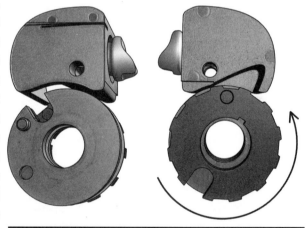

2ⁿᵈ Number - Rear & Middle Wheels Set

only the front wheel is keeping the lever in place and the bolt locked. As before, the front wheel has to rotate in the opposite direction, which is now clockwise again. This is so that the front wheel catch won't disturb the position of the middle wheel. Since the faceplate directly manipulates the front wheel, you can easily set it to the right position without turning one full revolution. In fact, if you turned it more then one full revolution, you would disturb the middle wheel. This is because the wheel catches would again

3rd Number - All Wheels Set

come into contact. Always remember that the notch location on the back wheel is associated with the first combination number. The middle wheel notch location is related to the second number, and the front wheel attached to the faceplate is associated with the third and last number in the combination.

You should now have almost the entire picture of how the lock works. There are still a few more details that will make the picture complete.

Let's take a look at a cutaway view of the bolt and lever. Notice that the bolt itself is spring-loaded. Also notice that the pin that goes through the hole also prevents the bolt from flying out of the housing. This pin not only gives something for the housing to rotate around, but also keeps everything together. The reason the bolt is spring-loaded inside the lever, which is spring-loaded itself, is to allow the shackle to close

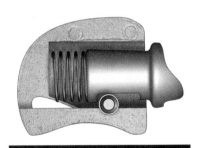

Spring Bolt inside Lever

without setting the combination. The shackle can simply be pushed into the lock, and the bolt will be pushed back. Once inserted, the bolt will spring out into the notch in the shackle and keep it in place. A common way of defeating older and poorly-manufactured locks is to simply push something thin into the lock to slide the bolt back into its housing, and therefore, allow the shackle to move out. Padlock shims are sold for this purpose. They need to be very thin and strong. Modern manufacturing and better locks have tighter tolerances to prevent this primitive method of lock picking.

Let's now put all the pieces together and examine this dissection of the entire combination lock. You should now have a clear idea of how a combination lock functions. We suggest that you purchase several combination locks so that you can take one of them apart and use the rest for practice. Often, the easiest way to disassemble one of these locks is to pry apart the metal that holds the backplate onto the lock.

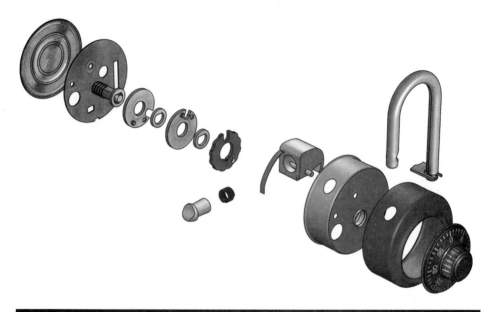

Combination Lock Parts

Combination Lock Faceplate

Cracking Combination Locks

You are now ready to learn the skills that will allow you to open many common combination padlocks without any prior knowledge of the true code. This technique may not apply to better, more sophisticated, and more expensive locks. The idea is to make your job of finding the correct combination as easy as possible. These combination locks usually have 40 numbers on their faceplates and come with three wheels, meaning that their combinations are composed of three numbers. In theory, three numbers with 40 possibilities each provides 40 x 40 x 40 = 64,000 total possible combinations. That would take a long time to try one by one. Don't worry yet. It should not be necessary to try every single one of these possibilities to open the lock. We will provide techniques you can use to be smart about which combinations to try in order to find the correct one much faster.

Picking a lock is usually a game against the manufacturing tolerances of the manufacturer; the same is true for combination locks. This means that for many locks, you can be either one or two numbers to the left or right of the true number. Note that the listed number in the published combination might not be the center number over the true gate. So it may be true that even if you are one number away from the published number, you may not be able to open the lock. But in those cases, extra numbers on the other side of the reported number might still work. This means that instead of dialing an exact number, it is possible to dial a whole range of neighboring numbers and the lock will still open. The numbers that come with the lock fall within these notch opening ranges. The numbers that are published may not necessarily be in the middle of the range. It is, in fact, very likely for some numbers to lie on the edge of the acceptable range. This makes it less obvious to observant individuals that only a fraction of all possible combinations need to be tried in order to find the combination.

In order to save on manufacturing costs, the middle and back wheels usually aren't manufactured in all 40 possible variations. There are, in fact, often only 10 variations of each wheel that you need to worry about. If you can determine where the center of the notches line up, then you can narrow the rear wheels to only 10 possible numbers each. There are also tricks you can use to find the third number much faster than trying each unique combination.

Ten Notch Wheels

Let us first consider the case where there are nine false notches and one correct notch on the front wheel. The front wheel could be attached to the faceplate with the true notch under any one of the 40 numbers. The center of the real notch could be at any one of those 40 different locations under each number. If you can find out where the centers of the false and real notches are, then you would at least be able to narrow down the options for where the real notch is

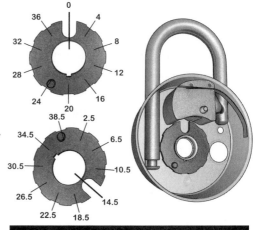

Example Notch Distributions

to just ten possibilities. That's a lot better than 40, and you are well on your way to reducing the possible combinations. You already know from the description of the combination lock that it's possible to tell when the bolt is stuck inside a notch. You might not be able to tell if it is a false or real notch, but just the knowledge of where the center of the notch is provides useful information about the lock.

First start by turning the faceplate three times counterclockwise. Stop rotating counterclockwise when you reach zero. This makes sure that when you make one faceplate rotation clockwise, you don't move any of the other wheels that might interfere with your notch readings. Next, pull on the shackle and start turning the faceplate clockwise until you reach your first notch (it doesn't matter if it's false or real). You will know that the bolt is stuck in a notch because it will be hard to move the faceplate much in either direction as long as tension is maintained on the shackle. Keep pulling on the shackle, turn clockwise as far as the faceplate will go, and remember that number; then turn counterclockwise as far as the faceplate will go and remember that number. These two numbers should have a very small difference between them. The number in the middle of those two numbers is the center of that notch. Relieve some pressure from the shackle so that you can skip over into the next notch. Once you are in the next notch, find out its center. Keep finding centers of notches until you go full circle and arrive at zero again. Your notch centers should be evenly spaced from each other. You should find ten or twelve notches. Some cheaper locks may only have 2 notches. More expensive or less common locks may even have different configurations, or may not have the notches evenly spaced at all. For now, we will continue describing the example with ten notches. The knowledge you gain here will still be useful when discussing those other lock styles.

Now that you have collected 10 notch center positions, you know the distribution of notch centers on the front wheel. The notch centers should be evenly distributed around the wheel. The following table presents 4 possible distributions of notches on the front wheel. Note that there are only 4 different distributions listed, not 40. That is because if the notch centers were rotated another number past the fourth distribution, it would look just like the first distribution, since the notches are evenly spaced. For this reason, every distribution is composed of unique notch centers. If you find that the notches are centerd in-between numbers, don't worry. Just pick the distribution that is closest, or add a half to each one. If the notch width did not allow the nearest integer to work, then the published combination of integers would also not work. You started with a total of 40 possible locations where the true notch could be. Once you figure out which column your distribution matches, then you have narrowed down the possibilities to only 10 locations. Remember that the true notch could be in any one of the ten positions of that distribution.

10 Gate Lock - 4 Different Notch Center Distributions

0	1	2	3
4	5	6	7
8	9	10	11
12	13	14	15
16	17	18	19
20	21	22	23
24	25	26	27
28	29	30	31
32	33	34	35
36	37	38	39

The centers of the possible notch positions on the rear wheels will usually match up with the distribution of possible notch locations you found for the front wheel. For example, if the distribution of notches on the front wheel was 0, 4, 8, 12, 16, 20, 24, 28, 32, and 26, then those would also be the possible numbers for the notches on the back wheel. The middle wheel is slightly different. When manipulating the middle wheel, the wheel catches will be touching the opposite sides of each other. That means you need to add the thickness of two wheel catches to each possible notch location for the second number. With this style of lock, that means adding 2 to each number. So the possible second numbers would be 2, 6, 10, 14, 18, 22, 26, 30, 34, and 38. The following table shows all of the possible combinations of the first and second number, which represent the back and middle wheel notches, for a particular distribution. Each distribution would have a different chart like this one. If the front wheel has notches centered on 1.5, 5.5, 9.5, 13.5, 17.5, 21.5, 25.5, 29.5, 33.5, and 37.5, then the chart would list them as possible locations of the back wheel and the middle wheel would have notches at 3.5, 7.5, 11.5, 15.5, 19.5, 23.5, 27.5, 31.5, 35.5, and 39.5.

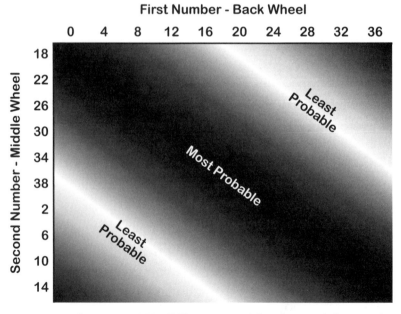

As you can see, there are 100 different combinations of first and second numbers: 10 possible locations of the first true notch times 10 possible locations of the second true notch. However, the first and second numbers can't be the same or too similar, or the wheel catches would engage on the other side and mess up the back wheel when you attempted to set the middle wheel. That removes at least 10 possibilities, maybe more, leaving you with 90 or less possible combinations: still a lot to try. To make your job easier, not all of the combinations of the first two numbers are equally likely. Many manufacturers prefer to separate the two notch positions by about half of a full rotation. This means that whatever the first number is, the second number is more likely to be on the other side of the dial. Therefore, if the first number is very high or low, then the second one will be near the middle. If the first number is in the middle of the number range, then the second will likely be at the high or low end of the number range. While such combinations may be more prevalent, manufacturers certainly don't want to make it too easy to crack their locks. Therefore, they will still make less likely combinations to keep us guessing. The chart here demonstrates the probability of each combination.

10 Gate Lock - First two numbers to try for dist. A

Try this first number...	Then try this second number...								
	Most Likely			------------------>				*Least Likely*	
0	18	14	22	10	26	6	30	2	34
4	22	18	26	14	30	10	34	6	38
8	26	22	30	18	34	14	38	10	2
12	30	26	34	22	38	18	2	14	6
16	34	30	38	26	2	22	6	18	10
20	38	34	2	30	6	26	10	22	14
24	2	38	6	34	10	30	14	26	18
28	6	2	10	38	14	34	18	30	22
32	10	6	14	2	18	38	22	34	26
36	14	10	18	6	22	2	26	38	30

When you are searching for the correct code, you should try the combinations of the first and second numbers that are most probable first, and then move on to less likely combinations. To use this table, first set the back wheel to the first number. Then look across the row to the right to see the possible second numbers you should try for the true notch in the middle wheel. Start by trying each row with the most probable columns, then going over each row again with less and less likely columns.

If, through one of the methods described later, you happen to know the third number, then you have an added bonus. Skip any combination with a second number similar to the third, and focus first on the rows which have a similar first number to the third number you already know. This table shows the various possibilities of the back and middle wheels for the first notch distribution: when the first notch center is at 0. You can find tables for all four different distributions at the end of this section. You can copy these tables so that you may cross off combinations to ignore similar second and third numbers and combinations that you have already tried.

Separately trying out each unique combination of the first two numbers is necessary. Finding the third number is much easier. You have already learned how to logically step through the most probable combinations of the back and middle wheels. After dialing each combination, you can quickly try out all of the remaining numbers of the front wheel. As you try each two-number combination, try all of the 9 possible third numbers with a single rotation of the front wheel. Trying 9 combinations of the third number quickly is a skill that, when mastered, will really speed up finding that elusive combination. There are really only 9 possibilities, not 10, since the second and third numbers can't be the same or just slightly higher.

This part of the job could take up most of your time. If the front wheel didn't have false notches, one could simply pull on the shackle and rotate the front wheel until the bolt sank into the notch. Unfortunately for us, life isn't quite so simple. It really helps to develop skills that compensate for the added difficulty of false notches. Learn to relieve some of the pressure off the shackle when the bolt housing and lever get stuck in a false notch. You must relieve just enough pressure to be able to skip over into the next notch, but not so much that you skip over an entire notch. Any notches you skip over could possibly be the correct one. With the mastery of this skill, you can quickly try out all the notches in the front wheel in one turn. For the purpose of training, you can buy various combination locks with 1, 9, or 11 false notches. Dial in the first two numbers on all of them and try to search for the third number without remembering it ahead of time. Try feeling out all of the false notches until you reach the correct true notch. You must learn how to balance the force applied to the shackle and the rotational force applied to the faceplate. In some ways, this skill of balancing two forces is similar to driving a stick shift, with the exception that you are using hands and not feet. With practice, this skill will save you most of the time that it takes to find the right combination.

There are some other tricks to help make it easier to test for the third number. As you pull on the shackle and rotate the faceplate, notice if the wheel turns with or without any friction. If there is resistance to turning the wheel while lifting on the shackle, then the lever must be scraping on a false notch that was cut shallower than those on the rear wheels. Since the wheel is attached directly to the faceplate dial, pressure from the shackle will push the lever into the front wheel and hold the dial in place with friction. That means that this notch is obviously false and there is no need to try it as a possible third number every time.

On the other hand, if the wheel turns smoothly, despite applying force to the shackle, then you do not know if the notch is the true one or not. When a false notch is cut deeper than those on the other wheels, it will feel indistinguishable from the true notch. If there is only one notch that behaves like this, you have just found the third number! Even if there are a few notches that do not stick, this knowledge is very useful. Pick one of these questionable notches and only test one of them for each set of first two numbers. If any of the front wheel notches allows the wheel to spin freely, then you know the first two numbers are not correct since the lever is binding on one of the rear wheels instead. Later, while trying a different combination, if this same notch resists wheel turning and "binds" when the shackle is pulled it will mean that the first two numbers are correct! After that, it should be a simple matter of trying all of the remaining possible true notches.

Sometimes your job will not be this easy. When the front wheel's outer diameter is actually smaller than the rear wheels you will not be able to feel any false gates. This is not common, however, because you could simply rotate all three wheels and feel for the slight interruptions that mark the notches in the rear wheels. The problem comes with finely-machined locks where the wheels are all roughly the same diameter. This makes it difficult to feel where the notches are. You may be able to feel some, but not all of them. Try jiggling the faceplate and angling it if you can. The best you may be able to get is slight changes in resistance as you spin the dial. Do the best you can and pick the distribution that is the closest match.

10 Gate Lock - First two numbers to try for dist. A

Try this first number...	Most Likely			Then try this second number... -------------------->				Least Likely	
0	18	14	22	10	26	6	30	2	34
4	22	18	26	14	30	10	34	6	38
8	26	22	30	18	34	14	38	10	2
12	30	26	34	22	38	18	2	14	6
16	34	30	38	26	2	22	6	18	10
20	38	34	2	30	6	26	10	22	14
24	2	38	6	34	10	30	14	26	18
28	6	2	10	38	14	34	18	30	22
32	10	6	14	2	18	38	22	34	26
36	14	10	18	6	22	2	26	38	30

10 Gate Lock - First two numbers to try for dist. B

Try this first number...	Most Likely			Then try this second number... -------------------->				Least Likely	
1	19	15	23	11	27	7	31	3	35
5	23	19	27	15	31	11	35	7	39
9	27	23	31	19	35	15	39	11	3
13	31	27	35	23	39	19	3	15	7
17	35	31	39	27	3	23	7	19	11
21	39	35	3	31	7	27	11	23	15
25	3	39	7	35	11	31	15	27	19
29	7	3	11	39	15	35	19	31	23
33	11	7	15	3	19	39	23	35	27
37	15	11	19	7	23	3	27	39	31

10 Gate Lock - First two numbers to try for dist. C

Try this first number...   Then try this second number...

Try this first number...	Most Likely			---------------->				Least Likely
2	20	16	24	12	28	8	32	4	36
6	24	20	28	16	32	12	36	8	0
10	28	24	32	20	36	16	0	12	4
14	32	28	36	24	0	20	4	16	8
18	36	32	0	28	4	24	8	20	12
22	0	36	4	32	8	28	12	24	16
26	4	0	8	36	12	32	16	28	20
30	8	4	12	0	16	36	20	32	24
34	12	8	16	4	20	0	24	36	28
38	16	12	20	8	24	4	28	0	32

10 Gate Lock - First two numbers to try for dist. D

Try this first number...   Then try this second number...

Try this first number...	Most Likely			---------------->				Least Likely
3	21	17	25	13	29	9	33	5	37
7	25	21	29	17	33	13	37	9	1
11	29	25	33	21	37	17	1	13	5
15	33	29	37	25	1	21	5	17	9
19	37	33	1	29	5	25	9	21	13
23	1	37	5	33	9	29	13	25	17
27	5	1	9	37	13	33	17	29	21
31	9	5	13	1	17	37	21	33	25
35	13	9	17	5	21	1	25	37	29
39	17	13	21	9	25	5	29	1	33

Summary

As you have learned earlier, with common locks of this type, there are 80 ways the faceplate could be connected to the front wheel under each number or half-number, though only 40 or less are important since integer numbers must operate the lock. This example lock has 4 notch distributions on that front wheel, with 10 possibilities for the true notch on all of the wheels for each distribution. Since you can tell which distribution your lock uses by feeling the notches, there really are only 10 possibilities for each number. That gave us 10 x 10 x 10 = 1,000 combinations to try. Because you can't have two of the same or similar numbers in a row, there are really only 9 possibilities for the second and third numbers. Therefore, you really only have 10 x 9 x 9 = 810 combinations to try. This is a lot better than 64,000! We improved on this with techniques to test just one third number for each set of first two numbers, and to try all possible third numbers with one spin of the dial. That brought us down to only 90 unique sets of first and second numbers. But we did even better still. Remember that you know that neighboring numbers in the combination are more likely separated by approximately a half rotation of the faceplate. Therefore, in order to be more likely than not of finding the correct first two numbers, you only need to check the 30 combinations in the first three columns of the most likely first and second numbers. Using these techniques, you might have only 30 sets of first and second numbers to be more than halfway sure of finding the correct combination!

Twelve Notch Wheels

To make their combination locks harder to crack, many locks have distributions of twelve notches on their front wheels, instead of just ten. With common locks of this type, the rear wheels are still only made with only 10 different possibilities each. Because the number of notches in the front wheel is different than the number of possible orientations of the true notch in the rear wheels, the technique to crack them is slightly backwards. We will start with the third number, and then try different sets of the first two numbers.

Twelve Notch Lock

As with common ten notch locks, the front wheel could be attached to the dial with the center of the true notch aligned under each number or half-number. Listed are 10 common distributions of the notches. The first step is to find which distribution of notches the front wheel has. Record the centers of each notch you find and match it up with one of the sample distributions. Because the rear wheels only have 10 possibilities each, the charts of first two-number combinations in the previous section will still work. We will discuss a faster technique later, but for now realize that the same simple approach with 10-notch locks should work here. The problem now is that just because you know the distribution of notches, you don't necessarily know which of the four charts to use. You will have to choose a third number first, and then use the matching dialing chart that contains that number as one of the possible first numbers. Try the different combinations of the first two numbers in turn with your chosen third number. If your chosen third number is correct, then you will find the correct combination in that chart. Otherwise, you may have chosen the wrong third number, and will have to repeat the process with a different third number and dialing chart.

12 Gate Lock - 10 Popular Notch Center Distributions

0.5	1.5	2.5	3.5	4.5	5.5	6.5	7.5	8.5	9.5
3.8	**4.8**	**5.8**	**6.8**	**7.8**	**8.8**	**9.8**	**10.8**	**11.8**	**12.8**
7.2	**8.2**	**9.2**	**10.2**	**11.2**	**12.2**	**13.2**	**14.2**	**15.2**	**16.2**
10.5	11.5	12.5	13.5	14.5	15.5	16.5	17.5	18.5	19.5
13.8	**14.8**	**15.8**	**16.8**	**17.8**	**18.8**	**19.8**	**20.8**	**21.8**	**22.8**
17.2	**18.2**	**19.2**	**20.2**	**21.2**	**22.2**	**23.2**	**24.2**	**25.2**	**26.2**
20.5	21.5	22.5	23.5	24.5	25.5	26.5	27.5	28.5	29.5
23.8	**24.8**	**25.8**	**26.8**	**27.8**	**28.8**	**29.8**	**30.8**	**31.8**	**32.8**
27.2	**28.2**	**29.2**	**30.2**	**31.2**	**32.2**	**33.2**	**34.2**	**35.2**	**36.2**
30.5	31.5	32.5	33.5	34.5	35.5	36.5	37.5	38.5	39.5
33.8	**34.8**	**35.8**	**36.8**	**37.8**	**38.8**	**39.8**	**0.8**	**1.8**	**2.8**
37.2	**38.2**	**39.2**	**0.2**	**1.2**	**2.2**	**3.2**	**4.2**	**5.2**	**6.2**

Fortunately, not all of the possible twelve notch locations are equally likely to be the third number. Notice that many of them are centered around half-numbers. Assuming that the notches are narrow enough, they cannot be possible third numbers since they would not cover an integer number. The numbers listed in bold are much more likely to be a real third number. Now take a closer look at the actual notch centers and widths that you recorded. Any notches that do not include an integer number, with enough leeway to be easy to dial, are not possible third numbers. Also, feel how easily the dial turns in each notch while the shackle is pulled. If there is any resistance against turning the dial while pulling the shackle in any of the notches, then the lever is pushing against a shallow false notch and you know it is not a possible third number. This should narrow the possible third numbers down to a manageable few. Now look for any notches that appear different. One that is offset from the pattern, perhaps, or maybe just wider than the rest. The true notch will often be unique somehow; if you are lucky, it will be obvious.

Here are 10 more possible notch distributions that lie in between the previous set of 10, and may come in handy with certain manufacturers. Different lock styles could even have different distributions with the 12 evenly spaced notches rotated by slight amounts.

12 Gate Lock - 10 More Notch Center Distributions

0.0	1.0	2.0	3.0	4.0	5.0	6.0	7.0	8.0	9.0
3.3	4.3	5.3	6.3	7.3	8.3	9.3	10.3	11.3	12.3
6.7	7.7	8.7	9.7	10.7	11.7	12.7	13.7	14.7	15.7
10.0	**11.0**	**12.0**	**13.0**	**14.0**	**15.0**	**16.0**	**17.0**	**18.0**	**19.0**
13.3	14.3	15.3	16.3	17.3	18.3	19.3	20.3	21.3	22.3
16.7	17.7	18.7	19.7	20.7	21.7	22.7	23.7	24.7	25.7
20.0	**21.0**	**22.0**	**23.0**	**24.0**	**25.0**	**26.0**	**27.0**	**28.0**	**29.0**
23.3	24.3	25.3	26.3	27.3	28.3	29.3	30.3	31.3	32.3
26.7	27.7	28.7	29.7	30.7	31.7	32.7	33.7	34.7	35.7
30.0	**31.0**	**32.0**	**33.0**	**34.0**	**35.0**	**36.0**	**37.0**	**38.0**	**39.0**
33.3	34.3	35.3	36.3	37.3	38.3	39.3	0.3	1.3	2.3
36.7	37.7	38.7	39.7	0.7	1.7	2.7	3.7	4.7	5.7

Once you have chosen a third number, select the dialing chart containing that number in the distribution of first numbers. You could try all of the combinations in that table, but you won't need to this time. Obviously, since you have already selected a third number, you only need to try that chosen third number, instead of all of them. That will save some time. To save more time, remember that the second and third numbers can't be too similar to each other. That means you can skip or cross off all possible sets of first and second numbers in the table where the second number is similar to your chosen third number. Finally, save more time by trying the more probable combinations first. That means focusing on the rows that have a similar first number as the chosen third number. When the correct third number is selected, then finding the combination is easier than the ten notch lock; otherwise it can take longer to try different third numbers.

To save even more time, there is an advanced dialing technique you can use. When using this approach, you do not need to individually dial each combination. Normally when entering a combination, you need to reset the wheels by spinning several times clockwise, set the first wheel, rotate once counterclockwise, set the second wheel, and then set the third wheel. That's a lot of spinning. When trying out many combinations with the same first and third number, you do not need to reset the wheels each time. Instead, you can go through the normal process with the first number you want to try. Then instead of resetting the wheels, keep the back wheel in place, and just adjust the middle wheel to a new number and try again. You should be able to try all of the different second numbers without touching the rear wheel.

The trick is to try the numbers in the correct order, so that you avoid disturbing the rear wheel. Let's run through an example to see how this is done. Suppose the chosen third number is 17. Start by resetting the wheels with three clockwise spins and then stopping at the first number to try for the first number, such as 1. Once the back wheel is set to 1, it should remain untouched while all of the combinations starting with 1 are tried. After setting the back wheel to 1, turn the dial counterclockwise once; then set the middle wheel to the second number possibility that is just higher than the first number. That is 3 in this case, which is just two digits higher than 1. After that, rotate clockwise to the chosen third number of 17 and try the shackle. You have just attempted 1-3-17. If this fails, do not reset the wheels. Instead, simply rotate the dial counterclockwise past 3 where the dial will engage with the middle wheel again, and move that middle wheel slightly further to the next possible second number of 7. When the middle wheel is moved into its new position, spin the dial slightly clockwise back to 17, and pull the shackle to test 1-7-17. Keep repeating this process, moving the middle wheel further and further each time to try 1-11-17, 1-15-17, 1-19-17, 1-23-17, 1-27-17, 1-31-17, and 1-35-17. Note that when you get to 1-15-17, the clockwise spin to 17 will almost be a complete rotation. Right after that, you will have to actually turn past 19 twice when setting the middle wheel. The combination after that will then only have a slight movement clockwise from 19 to 17. The turns to set the middle wheel should then only be a small turn counterclockwise for 1-23-17, with larger turns for each following number. This will happen whenever your sequence of second numbers crosses the chosen third number. 1-15-17 is actually not too likely a combination, since the third number is only slightly larger than the second. The wheel catches are likely to reengage and disturb the middle wheel when moving to 17. Therefore, you could skip this combination to save time. If you want to keep it simple, however, it is safe to go through the complete sequence. If none of those numbers work and you dialed correctly, then you know the combination does not begin with 1 and end with 17. Simply move on to the next first number to try by resetting all three wheels and repeating this process. If none of the first number possibilities work, then you may have to try a different third number.

Here is an example dialing chart for the chosen third number 17. Notice that 15 has been removed as a possible second number to save time. If there are multiple third numbers you want to try which fit in the same 10-notch distribution, you can always try them both as you go through this pattern.

12 Gate Lock - Example Dialing Chart for Third Number: 17

Try this first number...		Then try this second number...								Then try third number...
17	19	23	27	31	35	39	3	7	11	17
21	23	27	31	35	39	3	7	11		17
13	19	23	27	31	35	39	3	7		17
25	27	31	35	39	3	7	11	19		17
9	11	19	23	27	31	35	39	3		17
29	31	35	39	3	7	11	19	23		17
5	7	11	19	23	27	31	35	39		17
33	35	39	3	7	11	19	23	27		17
1	3	7	11	19	23	27	31	35		17
37	39	3	7	11	19	23	27	31		17

Following are four dialing charts to use when cracking 12-notch locks. To use them, first choose the appropriate chart with the chosen third number included in the set of possible first numbers. The first column represents all of the possible first numbers. Start with the number that is the same as the chosen third number and move outward up and down. When going through the second number possibilities, you can skip the second number that is just slightly less than the chosen third number.

12 Gate Lock - First two numbers to try for dist. A

Try this first
number...

Then try this second number...

Skip second number slightly less than third number

0	2	6	10	14	18	22	26	30	34
4	6	10	14	18	22	26	30	34	38
8	10	14	18	22	26	30	34	38	2
12	14	18	22	26	30	34	38	2	6
16	18	22	26	30	34	38	2	6	10
20	22	26	30	34	38	2	6	10	14
24	26	30	34	38	2	6	10	14	18
28	30	34	38	2	6	10	14	18	22
32	34	38	2	6	10	14	18	22	26
36	38	2	6	10	14	18	22	26	30

12 Gate Lock - First two numbers to try for dist. B

Try this first
number...

Then try this second number...

Skip second number slightly less than third number

1	3	7	11	15	19	23	27	31	35
5	7	11	15	19	23	27	31	35	39
9	11	15	19	23	27	31	35	39	3
13	15	19	23	27	31	35	39	3	7
17	19	23	27	31	35	39	3	7	11
21	23	27	31	35	39	3	7	11	15
25	27	31	35	39	3	7	11	15	19
29	31	35	39	3	7	11	15	19	23
33	35	39	3	7	11	15	19	23	27
37	39	3	7	11	15	19	23	27	31

12 Gate Lock - First two numbers to try for dist. C

Try this first number...

Then try this second number...

Skip second number slightly less than third number

2	4	8	12	16	20	24	28	32	36
6	8	12	16	20	24	28	32	36	0
10	12	16	20	24	28	32	36	0	4
14	16	20	24	28	32	36	0	4	8
18	20	24	28	32	36	0	4	8	12
22	24	28	32	36	0	4	8	12	16
26	28	32	36	0	4	8	12	16	20
30	32	36	0	4	8	12	16	20	24
34	36	0	4	8	12	16	20	24	28
38	0	4	8	12	16	20	24	28	32

12 Gate Lock - First two numbers to try for dist. D

Try this first number...

Then try this second number...

Skip second number slightly less than third number

3	5	9	13	17	21	25	29	33	37
7	9	13	17	21	25	29	33	37	1
11	13	17	21	25	29	33	37	1	5
15	17	21	25	29	33	37	1	5	9
19	21	25	29	33	37	1	5	9	13
23	25	29	33	37	1	5	9	13	17
27	29	33	37	1	5	9	13	17	21
31	33	37	1	5	9	13	17	21	25
35	37	1	5	9	13	17	21	25	29
39	1	5	9	13	17	21	25	29	33

One Notch Wheels

Sometimes, cheaper locks will have only one notch on the front wheel and no false notches at all. Often, as the picture depicts, they will have at least one false notch. When there is only one notch present, then it is easy to discover its center. To understand how the second false notch can complicate things, let us take a look at the shape of the false notch.

One Notch Lock

The false notches in these locks don't usually have a sharp drop off on both ends, but rather have one sloped side. The real notch still has steep edges on both sides. In this situation it is possible, with some difficulty, to rotate out of one side of a false notch while tension is applied to the shackle. When you are in the real notch, it is difficult to rotate the faceplate out of the notch in either direction while tension is being applied. This is how you can recognize when you are in the real notch.

Use a similar technique for cracking these locks as you did with the twelve notch locks. When looking for the third number, however, your job is much easier. This is because you no longer have many false notches preventing you from simply putting pressure on the shackle and rotating the front wheel. With this type of lock, you can freely spin the smooth wheel until the lever falls into the one false notch. Now you just have to release pressure on the shackle and let the lever jump to the next notch, which you know will be the correct one. Because this is so much easier to crack, you will only find this design on cheaper combination locks.

Once you find the center of the real notch, congratulations: you have just found the third number in the combination. You will still have to repeat the trial-and-error approach to discover the correct first two numbers. The procedure for finding the first two numbers should match the approach used with the twelve notch lock in the previous section. The difference is that you know for sure what the third number is.

Choose the chart of first two number combinations to try by picking the one with the known third number in the set of possible first numbers. As with the twelve notch lock, start with the most probable combinations of the first two numbers. Because you know the third number, focus on the rows with the similar first number as the known third number. This will further help you to find the correct combination sooner.

Wrap Up

There are other shortcuts to reduce the combinations you need to try. The above procedure assumed that the wheels were left in a random position. Lock users are supposed to spin the dial a few times after using them in order to reset the wheels in the lock. Sometimes people don't completely reset the wheels when they lock the combination lock. If you are lucky, the dial might still read close to what the third number is. Even if that is not the case, you can still take advantage of wheels that are not properly reset. Turn the front dial and wheel counterclockwise until you feel or hear when it engages the middle wheel. If the middle wheel was left in the correct position, then you have just found the second number in the combination. Continue to turn the dial and you will eventually feel the middle and back wheels engage. This represents the first number in the combination. These numbers might not be exact, as the wheels might rotate slightly as they engage, but they could be close and may help you try more likely combinations first. To prevent this, some locks have an auto-reset feature. This feature will slightly turn one or more wheels when the shackle is opened or reinserted.

For some locks, the false notches might not be the same size or evenly spaced. If that is all that is different, the approach described here should still work. First identify which of the notches are possible third numbers, and then use the advanced dialing technique to find the correct combination.

As always, more expensive and sophisticated locks will be much harder to defeat by trying combinations through brute force. If a manufacturer uses more random combinations, then the correct combination could be any of the possible sets of first and second numbers with equal probability. The charts in this book also assume the rear wheels are set in 10 different possibilities, 4 numbers apart each. If a lock type has a different distribution of possibilities, then the charts would have to be changed accordingly. If a lock is not of the common padlock style examined here, and you do not know the set of possible notch positions, then you will have to try more combinations to be sure of finding the correct one. If tolerances are poor enough, you may get by from trying just even or odd numbers. Still, be sure to use the advanced dialing technique described in the twelve notch section to speed up this process.

Sometimes manufacturers describe their combinations with left-right-left spins instead of the traditional right-left-right numbers. You can usually spin the wheel either left-right-left or right-left-right to get the lock to open. However, the numbers for the two approaches will be different due to the thickness of the wheel catches. This is particularly significant with narrow notches. A manufacturer might publish a left-right-left approach with the notches properly covering integer numbers. However, if the notches are narrow enough, and the wheel catches are an odd thickness, then rotating the wheels in the opposite directions may cause the true notches to not line up under an integer number. Generally though, all common locks will be provided with numbers meant to be used when spinning the wheel right-left-right.

Good luck using the techniques described in this book. As you can see, determining the right combination for a combination lock is quite different than picking a tumbler lock. Some aspects are always the same, though, such as the need for patience and persistence. These techniques are designed to take an insurmountably large set of possible combinations and reduce it to a manageable set of combinations to be tried. How long it takes will depend on your skill and the lock tolerances. Even for combination locks, practice is the key.

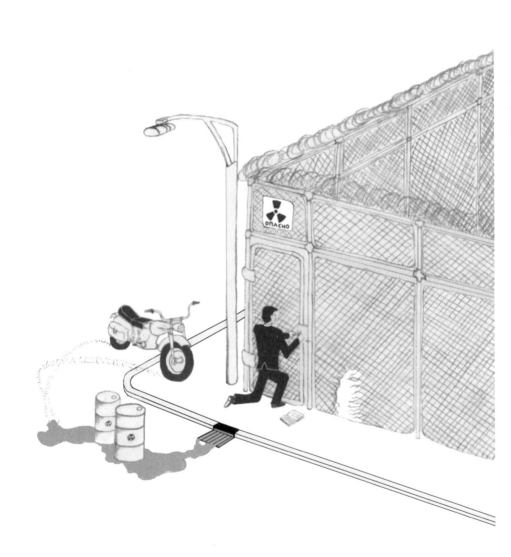

**Final
Rants**

Final Rants

This book has covered the most common locks that you are likely to encounter. Most of the locks in use are either one of these types or subtle variations thereof. However, they do come in a wide variety of shapes and sizes. With just a little bit of practice, anyone can defeat most common locks found on padlocks, house locks, desks, cabinets, etc... After trying these techniques, it is easy to lose faith in the common door lock. Becoming familiar with the ease of lock picking can initially give one an unprotected feeling. This same knowledge, however, can bring you peace of mind. You know better the appropriate security devices to obtain, as well as what assistance is necessary in a given situation. Higher-security cylinders may take a lot of practice and skill. While you may never be able to pick the best locks out there, you should be able to greatly expand your picking skills over time.

Locksmithing is an ancient trade. Ever since locks have been invented and used, our society has needed people to maintain those locks. In the past, medieval guilds and other types of locksmith associations, unions, and organizations were more prevalent. They closely guarded their secrets in order to be able to exploit their knowledge and charge well for their services. Strict control was kept over apprentices, lock technology, and bypass methods. Because they were so strict and held an almost monopolistic power, lock technology advanced very slowly. Today, although this information is much more accessible in trade publications, locksmiths are still able to charge quite well for their services. The coming of the information age has led to an explosion in the amount of information available. If you do choose to read about lock picking online, be very wary of your source. Although many such sources may be entertaining, they can also be misleading and/or wrong.

One thing that has survived through the ages is a sense of ethics among the professional locksmithing community. It is best to maintain this tradition and a high personal integrity. Locksmithing is an occupation that requires a variety of skills. This book does not go into detail about many important concepts, such as how to install a deadbolt, carpentry, machining, electronics, accounting, etc... As a locksmith, you can also get involved with dealing with various kinds of security systems. What you choose to pursue is really up to you. Your motivation is the only limiting factor of your success.

It is very important that you make certain that you have the proper authorization or permission to open a lock before you attempt to pick it. Also make sure that the person giving you permission is actually authorized to do so. It may be illegal for you to carry lock picking tools on your person. Make certain to verify local laws with respect to your situation. Keep in mind that people may hold you liable for damages if you destroy something while attempting to defeat a lock. Your local locksmith can be a valuable source of information.

Do not have an ego when approaching a lock or try to show off. Do not try to forcibly attack the lock. Instead, try to work with the lock. Cooperate with it, and it will cooperate with you. Patience is a critical skill to master. When you lose patience, there is little hope of succeeding. Take your time, don't rush, and listen to what the lock is telling you. This may sound unnecessary, but you are dealing with small metal objects machined to tight tolerances moving over distances that are indiscernible to the naked eye. You have to be finely tuned with all of your senses in order to understand what the lock is saying. With time and practice, you too can become a master locksmith.

In recent years, lock picking for sport has really grown in popularity. Participants never really pick locks attached to anything; they simply pick locks for the pure enjoyment of it. Sporting clubs, local groups, and even large competitions have started sprouting up. Germany in particular plays host to a large organized association. This book has even been translated into German due to the sport's popularity. There may be many lock picking aficionados in your area.

Glossary

Glossary

999 key – see *Bounce Key*

Actuator – In the lock picking context, an actuator is any device or component of a device that activates or deactivates a locking mechanism when operated.

Antipick latch – These latches are often found on door locks that can be closed without a key. It is a smaller secondary latch that sits next to the large, main latch. The main latch is spring-loaded, protrudes out of the door, and keeps the door closed. When the secondary latch is held depressed while the door is closed, it mechanically prevents the main latch from being retracted back into the door. Since the main latch cannot simply be pushed in, this latch design helps thwart shimming.

Barron's lever lock – A style of lever lock that raised the lever to match notches in the bolt, as opposed to modern lever locks which has notches in the lever instead.

Bevel - An angled edge. For example, most spring-loaded latches have a beveled edge to allow them to close without unlocking the lock. Holes can also be beveled to cause pins to false set on them.

Binding – Occurs when the hull and the plug crimp the pin, holding it in place.

Bit – The portion of the key that actually turns or actuates the locking bolt and/or makes contact with the tumblers.

Bitting – The configuration of the notches or cuts in the key that are made to match the lock.

Bitting depth – The depth of a notch on the key.

Bitting position – The location of a notch on the key.

Blade – The portion of a key that contains the notches and bitting.

Blank – A key that has not yet been cut or shaped to fit a lock.

Bolt post – The part of the bolt that can slide in and out of levers when the appropriate key is operating the lock.

Bottom pin – The lower pin in a pin cylinder that makes direct contact with the key. The key pins are cut at various heights to complement the depths of the key's notches.

Bounce key – A specially cut key with each notch cut to the deepest level. All that is left of the key's blade is a small ramp for each pin. As the key is rapped within the lock, each ramp bounces a pin to set them all simultaneously.

Bow – The handle of the key. The portion of the key that is held with the fingers.

Break a pin – see *Set a pin*

Bump key – see *Bounce key*

Bypass picking – The method of "picking" a lock whereby the lock is bypassed and the locking bolt is directly manipulated.

Case – see *Casing*

Case screw – The screw responsible for holding the lock's cover on.

Case ward – A portion of the case itself that acts as a ward. A key must be properly cut so as to avoid this obstruction.

Casing – The main structural portion of the lock. The plug rotates within the casing.

Chamber – The hole in the casing into which the plug is installed.

Changes – The number of keys a certain type of lock can differentiate between.

Clean opening – The act of skillfully opening a lock without damaging it or using force.

Combination lock – A lock design that uses no key. Instead, the user must remember and enter a combination to unlock the device.

Core – see *Plug*

Cuts – see *Notches*

Dead bolt – a bolt that is not beveled and is not spring-loaded. It may only be operated by locking or unlocking the lock directly.

Dead latch – see *Antipick latch*

Dead pin – A completely immobile pin instead of a normal moveable pin intended to prevent incorrect keys or picking tools from being used in the keyway.

Disc tumbler – see *Wafer tumbler*

Double-bitted disc tumbler – see *Double-sided wafer tumbler*

Double-custody lock – A lock that requires two different keys to be used simultaneously in order to open. Just one of the keys alone will not work.

Double-locking – A lock design that uses two distinct locking mechanisms that keep the lock closed. Both mechanisms must be unlocked for the overall device itself to open. Often found in handcuff designs.

Double-sided wafer tumbler – A wafer lock that has alternating springs that require some wafers to be pushed up while others need to be pushed down.

Driver pin – see *Top pin*

Driver spring – A spring at the top of the pin stack that pushes the pins or tumblers downward towards the keyway.

Electric pick gun – An automated pick gun.

End ward – A ward located at the end of the keyway. The key tip must be shaped to move around or to avoid this ward.

Faceplate – The dial on a combination lock with numbers printed on it that is rotated in order to dial the combination.

False notches – Notches on a lever or wheel designed to mimic a real notch when picking or cracking and prevent the lock from opening.

False set – When a pin gives the impression that it has set properly, but in reality it is still blocking the shear line.

Feelers – Sliding levers that go in and out of a tubular lock picking tool. When these levers are properly set, the tool mimics the shape of the actual key and can operate the lock.

Fence – see *Lever*

Floating pin – A pin that is able to move up and down freely.

Following tool – see *Plug follower*

Front trap - A cavity inside the lever of a lever lock. The bolt post rests within this cavity when the lock is locked.

Front wheel – The wheel nearest the dial faceplate in a combination lock. This wheel usually contains several false notches.

Gate – see *Wheel Notch*

Hook pick – A tool used to pick locks by manually manipulating each pin individually.

Hull – see *Casing*

Impact Picking – This picking method requires all of the bottom pins to be struck at the same time. These bottom pins transfer the momentum to the top pins, which fly above the shear line. This allows the plug to be turned at exactly that moment, opening the lock.

Impressioning – A method of creating a new key without the knowledge of what the original key looks like. Usually involves impressioning the shape or structure of the lock on a blank key and progressively filing it to work the lock.

Jiggler – see *Tryout key*

Key – A device designed to open one or more specific locks.

Key blank – see *Blank*

Key extractor – A tool used to extract broken key fragments or other small pieces from a lock's keyway.

Key pin – see *Bottom pin*

Keyhole – see *Keyway*

Keyway – The opening within the lock that the key is inserted into.

Latch – A bolt that extends out of the lock that enters the door frame, strike plate, shackle, or other entity that secures the lock shut.

Lever – A flat piece of metal in a lever lock that allows the bolt to slide into a notch only if the key rotates it the correct amount.

Lever – The part of the combination lock that rotates into the wheel notches and allows the lock to open.

Lever spacer – A flat piece that separate levers in a lever lock. They prevent the levers from disturbing each other while the key operates.

Lever tumbler lock – The type of lock with many levers inside of it. It is a very secure design when properly produced. Deposit boxes in banks often feature locks with more then 10 high-security levers inside of them.

Linus Yale – The inventor of the modern pin tumbler.

Lock – A device that attempts to prevent unauthorized access unless a pre-designated key, code, device, biometric, or other method of authentication is used.

Lock bypass – Opening a lock without using the intended key.

Locking bolt – The bolt that is directly actuated by the rotating action of the cylinder as the lock is locked/unlocked.

Lower pin – see *Bottom pin*

Master disc – see *Master pin*

Master key – A key that can open a set of different locks. These locks are designed to be opened by more than one type of key.

Master pin – A pin that lies between the top pin and the bottom pin. It creates more possible shear line combinations, meaning that more than one key can open the lock.

Master wafer – see *Master pin*

Middle pin – see *Master pin*

Mushroom driver – see *Mushroom pin*

Mushroom pin – A high-security pin designed to make picking more difficult by false setting.

Neck – The long portion of the key between the *bow* and the *stem*.

Notches – A cut in a lock component at a specific location or size.

Padlock – A portable lock with a shackle, loop, or other retaining component that may be attached to an object in order to secure it.

Pick – A tool of some fashion that may be used to manipulate tumblers or otherwise open a lock without the designated key(s).

Pick gun – A hand operated tool used for opening some pin tumbler locks intended to require minimal effort and skill.

Pins – Cylinder shaped pieces of metal that fit inside a lock and act as tumblers. Unless these pins are raised to an appropriate height, they prevent the plug from rotating.

Pin column – The stack of top, bottom, spring, and possibly master pins that slide within holes in pin tumbler locks.

Pin stack – see ***Pin column***

Pin tumbler – A lock design that utilizes pin stacks for their tumbler mechanism. The pins must be lifted to the proper height by the notches in a key such that they can separate at the shear line and allow the locking mechanism to turn.

Pivot hole – A hole inside of levers of a lever lock. A pin goes through these holes and allows the levers to rotate when the key is operated.

Plate wafer lock – A type of wafer lock that has many thin wafers, often as many as 15.

Plug – The inner cylinder of a lock. The portion of the lock that rotates when the key is turned. Many locks can have their plug removed for re-keying.

Plug follower – A tool that is used to push out a plug. It completely fills the void left by the plug and retains the top driver pins and springs within the hull and outer casing.

Plug holder – Tool used to hold a plug in place while performing maintenance on it.

Plug spinner – A tool used to quickly spin the plug. This tool can spin the plug so quickly that the top pins don't get the chance to drop into the plug.

Rake – A tool used to manipulate tumblers in order to unlock a lock without the designated key(s).

Raking – A method of unlocking several types of locks by directly manipulating its tumblers.

Rapping key – see *Bounce key*

Rear trap – The cavity inside the lever of a lever lock. The bolt post rests within this cavity when the lock is unlocked.

Re-key a lock – Rearranging or replacing the key pins with those of different heights such that a different arrangement of cuts is required for a key to work with the lock.

Reverse picking – A style of picking in which all of the top pins are pushed up past the shear line. The pin stacks are then raked and manipulated to cause the bottom pins to fall below the shear line.

Round tension tool – A round tool used to apply torque to both sides of a keyway. This style keeps the keyway clear and can help with double-sided locks.

Saddle – The curved part of the lever inside the lever lock that comes into contact with the key.

Scrubbing – see *Raking*

Security pins – Pins that are designed to make picking far more difficult.

Security tumblers – see *Security pins*

Serrated driver – see *Serrated pin*

Serrated pin – A type of security pin that has rough sides that catch on teeth inside the pin holes. This pin's configuration makes picking the lock more difficult.

Set a pin – To cause the division between the top and bottom pins to be at the shear line. When a pin is set, it will not prevent the plug from rotating.

Shackle – The metal loop of a padlock that can be attached to chains, gates, or whatever is being secured.

Shear line – The line of separation between the plug and the shell of the lock. When pins, discs, or other obstructions pass through this line, the core is unable to rotate. When this line is free of obstructions, the lock may be unlocked.

Shell – see ***Casing***

Shimming – Unlocking a lock by directly moving the locking bolt or latch. This method of opening locks avoids any manipulation of the tumblers or other locking mechanism.

Shoulder – The portion of the key that rests on the outside of the keyway when the key is fully inserted.

Sidebar wafer lock – A wafer lock which incorporates a bar that will only fall into place and allow the plug to turn once all of the wafer tumblers are aligned properly.

Skeleton key – A key for a warded lock that only has the parts needed to enter the lock and turn the bolt. There are no extra protrusions that could make contact with any wards and prevent the key from turning. This is in effect a master key for all warded locks of that type.

Snap gun – see ***Pick gun***

Spacer – An unmoving divider between levers in lever locks or wheels in combination locks that prevents neighboring levers or wheels from transferring motion to each other. A ***Master pin*** is also sometimes called a spacer.

Spacer washer –Small washers designed to stay still and prevent wheels inside of a combination lock from turning each other when their catches aren't touching.

Spool driver – see ***Spool pin***

Spool pin – A style of security pin that is wider on the top and the bottom. It is designed to false set, making picking more difficult.

Spring-loaded tension tool – A specialty torque wrench that allows for sensitive application of torque.

Stem – The portion of the key or pick that is usually a long thin piece of metal connecting the handle with the tip.

Strike plate – A plate, usually metal, often attached to the doorframe or other object. The lock's latch is designed to enter the strike plate to keep the lock shut.

Tailpiece – The actuator physically attached to the rear of the plug that is designed to move the locking bolt.

Tang – see *Stem*

Tension spring – A spring that presses the wheels and spacers together in a combination lock. This friction holds the wheels in place, allowing them to be placed and held in a specific position to open the lock.

Tension wrench – see *Torque wrench*

Thin-key pin – A slightly thin pin which is used as an anti-picking measure in tubular and lever locks.

Throat cut – A designed cut in a flat key that allows the trunnion to block the keyway to better prevent picking.

Tip – The end of the tool or key that enters the keyway first. In the case of a pick or rake it is the part that makes direct contact with and manipulates the tumblers.

Top pin – The upper pin in the pin cylinder that is pushed up into the hull when the key is inserted. The driver pin makes direct contact with the spring and "drives" the key pin below it downward.

Torque – A rotational force

Torque wrench – A tool that is inserted into the keyway and used to apply a rotational force on the plug.

Torsion wrench – see *Torque wrench*

Trap – see *Rear trap*

Trunnion – The part of the lever lock that encases the key while the lock is properly operated. It may help transfer rotational energy and block the keyway to impair lever manipulation.

Tryout key – A key that when jiggled in a lock will open a significant subset of a particular type of lock.

Tubular decoder tool – A tool used to measure the depths of the feelers on a tubular lock pick.

Tubular lock – A lock design that in principle is very similar to a pin tumbler except for the fact that the pin stacks are arranged in a circle instead of a line.

Tubular lock pick – A tool specifically designed to manipulate the pins of a round tubular lock.

Tumbler – The pins, wafers, discs, levers, or other objects that are moved or rotated a varying amount, depending on the key used. The lock will only unlock when the tumblers are moved an appropriate amount in the appropriate direction.

Turning tool – see *Torque wrench*

Turning wrench – see *Torque wrench*

Upper pin – see *Top pin*

Vibration picking – A method of opening a lock by bouncing the pins up and down until the shear line is clear and the lock is free to open.

Vice-grip – A hand tool that operates much like pliers, but can lock in place.

Wafer tumbler – A tumbler lock that uses disks instead of pins. There are many parallel discs inside the lock that line up with corresponding cuts in the key. The discs move in relation to the height of notches cut in a key. Only notches of the correct height will move the tumblers properly and allow the plug to rotate.

Ward – An obstruction that prevents an incorrect key from entering, rotating, or moving within a lock.

Warded lock – A lock design that utilizes wards to differentiate between keys and to only allow the correct key to operate the lock.

Wheel – A round flat disc in a combination lock. There are several wheels in a lock, each one rotates and has a notch that must be aligned properly for the lock to open.

Wheel catches –Protrusions on wheels inside combination locks. These protrusions touch and transfer rotation from one wheel to another. This allows the operator to properly position all of the wheels by dialing the right combination.

Wheel notch – A groove in a wheel of a combination lock. When all the notches of all the wheels align under the lever then the lock can properly open.

Wheel spacer – see *Spacer washer*

LEGAL NOTICE

You've read the book...
Now get the DVD!

The DVD version of this book takes the cutaway diagrams, and brings them to life with full color computer graphics! The video covers warded locks, pin tumbers, wafer locks, and explains several different picking techniques. This video is the perfect companion to the *Visual Guide to Lock Picking* to help you learn the art of lock picking.

Quickly reinforce the secrets from the Visual Guide with this video's concise, yet informative style. By practicing and applying the methods introduced, it is possible to master the picking of most modern locks. Starting with the basics, the video guide even includes master keys and high security pints. Now, not only can you see all of the moving parts, you can see them move. This dissection of the locks make it easy to see how they work. Step-by-step instructions are given for picking each type of lock. You will be lead through the entire process, introducing the necessary tools and covering several techniques leading you to that satisfying click as the lock springs open!

Also available in VHS.

Visual Guide to
Lock Picking

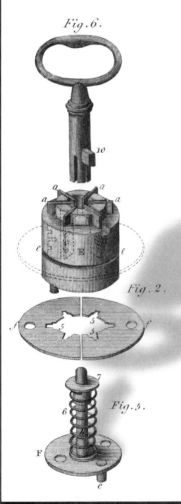

Fig. 6.

Fig. 2.

Fig. 5.

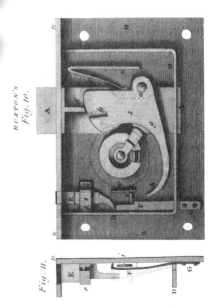

RUXTON'S Fig. 10.

Fig. 11.

3D ANIMATION

WARDED LOCKS

PIN TUMBLER LOCKS

WAFER LOCKS

AND MUCH MORE

www.StandardPublications.com

standard publications, inc.

VISUAL GUIDE TO **LOCK PICKING**

3rd Edition

Quick Order Form

___ DVD: **$39**^{95}

___ Third Edition: **$24**^{95}

___ Second German Edition: **$24**^{95}
(plus 7.5% tax in IL)

You may order instantly on the web:
www.StandardPublications.com
Or use this easy order form to order by mail. Include $3 extra if you want us to send it Priority.

Name	
Email	
Telephone	
Address	
City, State ZIP	

☐ Credit Card   ☐ Check/Money Order

Credit Card Number	
Expiration Date	
Signature	

Standard Publications, Inc.
Please Mail to: PO Box 2226
Champaign, IL 61825